# How I Topped the UPSC and How You Can Too

# How I Topped the UPSC and How You Can Too

What It Really Takes to Crack the World's Toughest Exam

Gamini Singla

JUGGERNAUT BOOKS
C-I-128, First Floor, Sangam Vihar, Near Holi Chowk,
New Delhi 110 080, India

First published by Juggernaut Books 2022

Copyright © Gamini Singla 2022

10 9 8 7 6 5 4 3 2

P-ISBN: 9789393986542
E-ISBN: 9789393986559

The views and opinions expressed in this book are the author's own. The facts contained herein were reported to be true as on the date of publication by the author to the publishers of the book, and the publishers are not in any way liable for their accuracy or veracity.

All rights reserved. No part of this publication may be reproduced, transmitted, or stored in a retrieval system in any form or by any means without the written permission of the publisher.

Typeset in Adobe Caslon Pro by R. Ajith Kumar, Noida

Printed at Thomson Press India Ltd

*For my late grandfather, Sh. Tarsem Kumar Singla, whose unflinching support, guidance and blessings have made me the person I am today! This book wouldn't be possible without your blessings. Miss you every single day.*

*Pillars of strength (left to right): My mother, father and brother, Tushar*

# Contents

| | |
|---|---:|
| Introduction | 1 |
| A Note about the UPSC CSE | 9 |

## Part 1: Crossing the Mental Hurdles

| | | |
|---|---|---:|
| 1. | How to Keep Yourself from Going Crazy with Comparisons | 17 |
| 2. | Why Being Fit Is Going to Help You Score | 26 |
| 3. | How to Take Risks and Win | 30 |
| 4. | How I Decided I Would Do the UPSC | 35 |
| 5. | Handling the Pressure from Your Family | 42 |
| 6. | I Just Can't Do It: Managing Stress | 53 |
| 7. | How Important Are Backups? | 62 |
| 8. | How to Make Sacrifices | 66 |
| 9. | Guilt | 72 |
| 10. | Change the Way You Talk to Yourself | 75 |
| 11. | When Everything Is Planned, Where Does Uniqueness Fit? | 81 |
| 12. | How Important Is It to Plan Well and Stay Consistent? | 86 |
| 13. | Happiness – An Important Accompaniment for Struggle | 90 |

## Contents

| | |
|---|---|
| 14. Have a 'No Excuses' Policy | 95 |
| 15. Dealing with Tragedies beyond Your Control | 102 |
| 16. How It Feels to Fail and Then Finally Succeed | 109 |

### Part 2: Rules of the Game

| | |
|---|---|
| 1. How I Planned for My First Prelims – And What I Got Wrong | 117 |
| 2. My Plan 2.0 Post Prelims | 123 |
| 3. How Many Hours of Study Do You Need?: A Sneak Peek into My Timetable | 134 |
| 4. How to Plan Your Breaks | 141 |
| 5. How Important Is It to Solve Mocks? | 145 |
| 6. How to Read Newspapers Effectively | 156 |
| 7. What to Do One Day before the Prelims | 161 |
| 8. What to Do to Get That Extra Edge in the Mains | 170 |
| 9. How to Ace the Optional Subject | 176 |
| 10. How to Use the Two and a Half Months after the Prelims | 180 |
| 11. How to Use the Two Hours between the Two Mains Papers | 183 |
| 12. Acing the Interview Stage | 186 |
| *Epilogue* | 191 |
| *Appendix* | 193 |
| *Acknowledgements* | 198 |
| *A Note on the Author* | 200 |

# Introduction

Hi, everyone. I am Gamini Singla and I'm 23 years old. I cleared the 2021 civil services examination (CSE) conducted by the Union Public Service Commission (UPSC) with an all India third rank. By the time this book is published, I would have joined the Indian Administrative Services and nearly completed my foundation course at the Lal Bahadur Shastri National Academy of Administration (LBSNAA), Mussoorie.

Let me quickly tell you my story. I was born in Bathinda, Punjab, my maternal home. My father belongs to Sunam, a small town in Sangrur, a district in Punjab. My parents are both government doctors based in Himachal Pradesh. I spent my pre-school years in Talwara, another small town in Punjab that borders Himachal Pradesh, where my parents were posted at a Primary Health Centre.

When my parents were transferred from Talwara, my primary schooling began in an even smaller town – almost a village – in Kangra district, near the government hospital

## Introduction

where my parents worked. When I entered class 5, my parents got transferred to a place in Bilaspur district. Since there were no good schools nearby, my younger brother and I were sent to Sunam (where my paternal grandparents lived), and I completed my class 5 there.

After that, my parents were transferred to Tehsil Shri Naina Devi Ji, and their hospitals were situated near the area bordering Punjab. I did my secondary schooling at Mount Carmel School, a convent offering the ICSE board near Anandpur Sahib, where we lived. Finally, it was here that my brother and I got a lot of exposure.

As our board was ICSE, there weren't enough holidays between our exams, and the syllabus was also quite vast. We developed the habit of studying a lot in a short span of time. I also participated in extracurricular activities like declamation contests, compering, debates and dance programmes. I managed to score 92 per cent in class 10 and was third in my class. I think the number 3 made a special place in my life then itself.

I heard about the civil services from my father during my childhood. He used to tell me about the responsibilities, authority and power of an Indian Administrative Services (IAS) officer. He would narrate stories of officers doing great work, utilizing their position to bring a positive change in society. As a kid, it fascinated me and I dreamt of becoming like them. Every time our class teacher asked

## Introduction

us about our aim in life, I would shout out loud, 'I want to be an IAS officer,' without knowing what it takes to reach there.

Then came the time to choose my academic stream for class 11. I definitely didn't want to pursue medicine as I thought it would limit me to just one field. One option was to take arts, as I had always dreamt of joining the civil services. But as my parents did not want me to lose a connection with science so early in life, we eventually decided on engineering after a lot of discussions!

I shifted to Chandigarh and started taking coaching classes for the formidable Indian Institute of Technology-Joint Entrance Examination (IIT-JEE). The **Joint Entrance Examination (JEE)** is an engineering entrance assessment conducted for admission to various engineering colleges in India. It is made up of two different examinations: the **JEE Main** and the **JEE Advanced** (only those who pass the JEE Main can sit for the Advanced). Though I cleared the JEE Advanced exam too, my rank was not good enough to gain admission to the topmost IITs.

So I chose to pursue computer science engineering at Punjab Engineering College (PEC) in Chandigarh. I joined in 2015 and was in the college hostel. In hindsight, it was a great decision. It was close to home, and Chandigarh is a beautiful city to spend your college years in.

## Introduction

After studying non-stop for two years, one needs a change too! I decided to explore different aspects of college life. I picked up my childhood hobbies, debating and public speaking, and added a particular love of mine – participating in Model United Nations. It was here that I developed the habit of daily 'newspaper reading'.

The CSE (note that technically the exam is called the CSE but colloquially it is also referred to as the UPSC exam. In this book, I'll use both the terms) conducted by UPSC was never far from my mind. So, during one break in my second year of college, I decided to seriously look at the syllabus for the exam. I took guidance from a local teacher in Patiala to get a gist of the subjects and to see whether it was my cup of tea. I really enjoyed those two and a half months of preparation.

After my vacation, I got busy and could not think about the UPSC exam. I had to prepare for my college internships, and when I bagged one, I decided to wait until I had experienced the corporate world before committing to the UPSC.

In January 2018, I went to Mumbai for a five-month internship as a junior finance analyst at J.P. Morgan Chase & Co., an American multinational investment bank and financial services holding company headquartered in New York City. As of 2022, J.P. Morgan Chase is the largest bank in the United States, the world's largest bank by

## Introduction

market capitalization and the fifth largest bank in the world in terms of total assets.

It was there that I realized civil services was my ultimate calling. In the book, I have discussed in detail the factors and my mindset that led me to this decision.

When I returned to college in June 2018, I started preparing for the CSE wholeheartedly and used my fourth and final year to prepare. At the time, I also received an offer from J.P. Morgan to join them as a full-time employee. I made up my mind to not join and go full steam ahead in preparing for the CSE.

So, in 2019, on the last day of my college, I went straight from Chandigarh to Patiala to prepare under the guidance of the same teacher I had consulted two years earlier.

I attended the morning classes at 5.30 a.m. daily and came back at about 11 a.m. after the optional class. After a 10-month stay at Patiala, I returned home in March 2020 when the lockdown was imposed due to the COVID-19 pandemic.

As I prepared at home, I started feeling that self-study was more productive; from March 2020 until the final results (over two years later), I stayed home and prepared solely through self-study and a few online test series.

In October 2020, I appeared for my first Prelims and failed miserably, with a score of just 66.5 out of 200. It was 26 marks less than the cutoff. In October 2021, I appeared again and, this time, cleared all the three stages with a top rank. The results were declared on 30 May 2022, the day that will always hold a special place in my heart.

## So why am I writing this book and why should you read it?

When I achieved a top rank, I received many requests to share my strategy, timetable and other aspects of my preparation. I was invited to give several talks to both aspirants and non-aspirants. However, a two or three hours' talk cannot capture the nitty-gritty details of a three-year-long rigorous preparation.

There were messages from youngsters across India from different educational backgrounds pursuing varied careers. Most of the questions were about dealing with mental hurdles one faces in a long, tiring, risky and uncertain journey. Many asked if coaching in a metropolitan city is a must even for a rural or poor but hardworking student.

I felt that there is a dearth of books that discuss this mental aspect of the journey in detail. This is despite mental preparation being the one common denominator to crack any competitive exam, be it UPSC, JEE, the National Eligibility cum Entrance Test (NEET), the Common Law Admission Test (CLAT), even your class 10 and 12 exams, the Master of Business Administration (MBA) entrance exam, corporate interviews and several others.

Introduction

When I struggled with issues like fear, uncertainty, demotivation, comparisons and failures during preparation, I wished for someone who could tell me that it was okay to face all this. I had to create strategies to help me deal with the tension, which I would like to share with you through this book.

The first part of the book deals with the mental struggles you may face on any path to success, where I will provide anecdotes from my journey. I'll tell you as honestly as I can how I sharpened my mental axe. Whatever exam you may take, I believe you will find tips and advice of value here.

Though mental toughness is a major part of the battle, there are certain rules of the game for cracking competitive exams. **Having failed the same exam by a huge margin and then been successful the second time, I have spent time thinking about not just why and how I succeeded but also why I failed initially**. I know the wrong lessons and prejudices that I unlearnt, and the new lessons I embraced, which were both essential to converting this failure to success.

The second part is about 'the unavoidable rules of the game' that I followed to crack CSE. Though I have written it focusing on the UPSC examination, similar variations of the rules apply to most competitive exams.

The syllabus and the exam pattern might be different, but ultimately what determines your success and failure is

## Introduction

the strategy involving proper planning, hard work coupled with smart work, a lot of practice, controlling your nerves on the day of the exam and many other tips.

Writing a book was not an easy task for me. I had never even thought about it. But here I am writing one – just a few months after my results and before the foundation course starts at LBSNAA. This book made me do what I had not done even during the CSE preparation – steal some time from my sleep to finish it on time!

My aim is to be of some help to those struggling alone in their journey, who work harder than most and still cannot get through. In this book I have included all the principles and mantras that worked for me. There are hundreds and thousands of ways to attain a goal – I can tell you what worked for me in the hope that it helps you to find your own path. I request you not to follow my path blindly but rather pick and choose what works for you best.

I will be deeply satisfied if I can be of some help to any one of you, even in a small way. I hope you enjoy and benefit from reading this book.

# A Note about the UPSC CSE

I'll be referring to the various papers and phases of the exam – most of you will know this, but here is a brief note for those who don't.

There are three stages in the UPSC Civil Services Exam:

1. Preliminary Exam (Prelims – Objective Test)
2. Mains Exam (Written Test)
3. Personality Test (Interview)

## Stage 1: Prelims

In 2021, around 10 lakh candidates applied to appear in the Civil Services Preliminary exam and only 9,214 candidates, i.e., less than 1 per cent (the lowest number in the last eight years) cleared this stage and became eligible for the second stage. The preliminary stage comprises two compulsory papers of 200 marks each: General Studies Paper 1, or GS 1, and General Studies Paper 2, or GS 2,

## A Note about the UPSC CSE

(also called the Civil Services Aptitude Test, or CSAT). The questions in the Prelims are multiple-choice questions (MCQs). The GS 1 has 100 questions carrying 2 marks each and the CSAT has 80 questions carrying 2.5 marks each. There is 'negative marking' in the Prelims for each incorrect answer and it is one-third of the allotted marks for the question. The CSAT is a qualifying exam, and candidates should score a minimum of 33 per cent in it. It's only when this cutoff is cleared that the GS 1 paper will be evaluated. The marks scored by the candidates in the Prelims are not counted for the final score. It is only a screening test where candidates not securing above the cutoff marks are eliminated. The cutoff for GS 1 exam varies each year as per the vacancies and difficulty level of the exam. In the 2021 Prelims, the cutoff score for General Category was 87.54 out of 200, one of the lowest in recent years as the exam was tough.

## Stage 2: Mains

The written examination (Mains) consists of nine papers, but only seven are counted for the final merit ranking. The remaining two papers are compulsory language papers of 300 marks each. The candidate has to secure a minimum of 25 per cent marks in these two language papers.

The seven papers are all three hours long and carry 250

## A Note about the UPSC CSE

marks each. The total weightage of the Mains examination is 1,750 marks. Five of these papers are common for all candidates, and two are optional papers chosen by the candidate from the list of subjects given by the UPSC. I chose sociology as my optional subject.

In 2021, of the 9,214 candidates selected for the Prelims examination, 1,824 made it to the Interview stage.

## Stage 3: Personality test

This final stage is for 275 marks. When added to 1,750 marks of the Mains, it takes the grand total marks to 2,025. The candidate is interviewed by an esteemed panel for about 30–40 minutes at the UPSC Bhavan, New Delhi. In 2021, out of 1,824 candidates, 685 made it to the final list.

Those who clear all the three stages of the UPSC CSE enter the prestigious civil services of the country and become officers in the IAS, Indian Foreign Service (IFS), Indian Police Service (IPS) and a host of other services.

# Part 1

# Crossing the Mental Hurdles

To pass any competitive exam, you have to train for two things. The first, of course, is the exam and the subjects. The second training involves your mind. The big difference between the time I failed my UPSC and when I cleared it was my mental toughness. You need to be strong to study hard, to not feel envious of your friends who are having fun while you're at your study desk. And you need to be even stronger when you face your exam papers and your mind goes blank in panic.

**I think the big difference between those who make it and the ones who don't, despite putting in the same hard work, is how mentally prepared they are**.

# 1

# How to Keep Yourself from Going Crazy with Comparisons

Are comparisons avoidable?
How do we stop comparing ourselves to our peers?
Is it even possible to not envy other people's success?

I used to be troubled by these questions. Most of us have a horrible habit of comparing ourselves with our peers – let's admit it, obsessing is the right word – who seem to be having a brilliant time while we struggle.

Of course, our mind is smart enough to trick us by just focusing on the good things about others and the bad things about us. In our envy, we forget to see the whole picture, the difficulties, the challenges and the sacrifices that the others have made and continue to make to get to where they are. We want the taste of strawberries while we buy guavas. Thus, we unknowingly enter a phase of self-pity and envy, which eats away at our efficiency until we finally lose the vigour and vitality for the big game.

## No social media

In 2019, at the age of 20, I left an extremely well-paying multinational company to prepare for my UPSC exam. While I slogged away for hours in my room, the thought of 'what I could have enjoyed instead' often crossed my mind. All my friends were working in MNCs, some were getting promoted, some were moving abroad to Canada, USA and UK. Others had got admissions to the top universities of the world and here I was struggling with an 'All Zero or Hero' process. It felt a little unfair that despite putting in double the efforts of my peers, I was not getting even half the results.

It's okay to feel this way – most of us have felt this combination of envy and insecurity. But what is not okay is to let it affect your determination and focus.

The first step in dealing with it is to shut off knowing what others are achieving – as much as possible. I was not on any social media platform, and I think it played a huge role in keeping my mind stable, allowing me to focus on my own performance. Sometimes, we feel that it only costs 10 minutes to scroll through our Instagram or Facebook feed. But I think the after-effects of those

10 short minutes are huge. It takes so much time to get yourself out of that zone of comparison. So why board a train going to a different destination?

But sometimes, comparisons are inevitable no matter what you do to shut out the outside noise. You can't, for example, shut off your closest friends or siblings you talk to regularly. In the process, you are unnecessarily putting your mind through unwarranted confusion and mental trauma. And an unsure, undetermined and unclear mind can never yield the best results. Reorient and remind yourself that you have consciously made a different choice and that frequent comparisons only lower your self-confidence.

Finally, I realized that what I envied was not what I wished for myself. Whether you pursue the CSE or JEE or NEET or CLAT, comparing your life with an old friend who chose an altogether different path is futile. It's a simple idea, but once I understood it, my whole attitude towards my peers and their achievements changed.

If it is still difficult, do a simple exercise. Just imagine exchanging your life with the other person, and visualize yourself in their position. Make sure you think about that person's complete life, both the good and bad aspects, like a composite package offer. If you are fine with both and you still crave your friend's position, then maybe you are in the wrong place, and you must give more time to deciding what you want. Every time I did this exercise, I came to the conclusion that I would not exchange my life with anyone else's, despite all the challenges or difficulties. You should be happy and proud that you had the courage to forego it and did not rush to pluck the low-hanging fruit. Remember: APNA TIME AAYEGA! (Our time will come!)

It is also important whom you compare yourself to. Usually, we tend to compare our paths with those we know, rather than those whose achievements we want to emulate.

## How not to let our competitors stress us out

We often compare our strategy, timetable, book list, study hours and so on with that of a fellow aspirant. We somehow feel that everyone except us possesses a magic wand. Rather than believing in ourselves, we start putting ourselves down. It harms us in two ways.

One, we unnecessarily start questioning our approach and invite self-doubt. Two, we make blunders by trying to copy others. I purposely did not join any aspirants, group on Telegram or WhatsApp. I was in touch with only two or three fellow aspirants. Studying in a group did not work for me, and I never felt the need to connect with any other aspirant. I liked to chalk out my own strategy and never discussed the books or test series that others were following.

Looking at it another way: Why follow someone whose path has yet not been tested? After all, the probability of their success is the same as yours.

However, what I have realized after interacting with numerous toppers is that everyone has a different temperament, different modes of working, pace of learning and ways of memorizing the same stuff. If we start imitating others, we just reduce our chances of success. So, analyse your strengths and weaknesses and then decide. If you feel that you need a companion to discuss important topics, and doing so keeps you more optimistic, go for it. I have seen my friends clearing the exam with the help of group study and discussions.

## But then, how do we know whether we are on the right path?

The answer is by constantly evaluating yourself vis-à-vis the ones who have already been through the same process and emerged victorious. In my first attempt, I was blindly following my own path, living in a shell. I made no effort to evaluate myself against the toppers.

In my first UPSC Prelims, I panicked when I realized that I could answer only 35 questions correctly and mentally lost the game there. When I listened to some topper videos after my first attempt, I realized that everyone actually knows only 35–40 questions, and the rest is calculated guesswork. Had I known this before, I would not have been afraid to guess some of the answers.

So if I had spared some time listening to the mistakes other toppers made, I might have been able to avoid them myself.

While preparing for my second attempt, I took note of strategies, book lists and timetables of multiple toppers and used their inputs to prepare my own strategy. As they say, suno sabki, karo man ki (hear out others, but do as you wish).

## Don't compare, learn to evaluate

Now you might be thinking, but who should I be listening to? There are so many videos and blogs by successful candidates with advice. But many contradict each other. Some say it is important to read newspapers, while others have cleared the exam using a current affairs compilation. Some gave 60 mock exams, and some got through with 20. Some studied for nine hours every day, but others put in just five hours. It gets a bit confusing here.

My approach was to listen to everything and arrive at the common denominators. For example, if you listen to

30 toppers from different years, you will find that at least 25 emphasize reading newspapers thoroughly. The same applies to the number of hours they put in. Most of them quote at least seven to eight hours. So the rule is to go with the common denominators – that's the best way to separate the signal from all the noise. Never ever idolize the exceptions. If one out of 20 achievers talks about an approach that seems either too easy or too difficult, it's better to drop it and go with the majority. Do not look for an easy formula or a path that bypasses hard work.

I kept a diary and every time I heard a topper's interview, I noted down everything relevant. Then I compared all of them and reached some common factors and followed them religiously. Once you do this exercise, avoid listening to everything that comes on YouTube or other social media platforms. It unnecessarily disturbs the mind. If I was ever confused, I would return to those notes I had made rather than listen to new content.

Lastly, don't forget your own personality, your strengths and your weaknesses. Do not blindly imitate toppers, but rather learn from them. Do not start waking up early just because some other achiever did so when you know that your best comes out at night. Do not force yourself to sit for two hours if your body allows only an hour at a time. Find your way to compensate – that's where you can show your creativity.

To conclude: Comparisons are harmful when done at the wrong time with the wrong person. Find the common denominator across multiple people (who have already achieved what you aspire to) and then apply it to yourself, customizing it as per your personality.

## Have you lost your mojo?

Now let's talk about comparisons with our own self. Often, we are too harsh on ourselves. Having been a good student all my life, I found it very difficult to accept failure during my first UPSC Prelims exam. Today I know that it's normal to feel that way. Human tendency is to feel that either we are not good enough or that we are not made for this, or that we have lost the spark. I felt I had forgotten what it was to achieve my dreams and that it was the end of the road for me. When I passed my second attempt, I realized it is neither about the spark nor about one's capabilities. It was about having tenacity and being patient. One way to stay motivated is to use your previous achievements as a booster and remind yourself constantly how you overcame tough times in the past.

The key lesson here is to make it a point to be a better version of yourself every single day. Compare today only with yesterday and try to walk the extra mile.

P.S.: If you think I have become a pro in managing envy and being unstressed by comparisons, you are mistaken. These thoughts still cross my mind, but the only difference is that with practice, I can quash them as soon as they appear. So don't be guilty about it; just keep trying until you finally overpower the emotion.

# 2

# Why Being Fit Is Going to Help You Score

I know most of you are confused and wondering about the relationship between exam success and health choices. But they are directly linked.

It's only when both the mind and body work in unison that we can reach our maximum potential. I have seen people talking about the need for adequate breaks for the mind, but very few people talk about our bodies needing a break too. If, after two hours of sitting at your desk, you watch an hour of TV, you might be able to relax the mind but you would be doing a grave injustice to your body. Relaxation for the body is as essential as it is for the mind.

## Two simple rules

One, I made sure I followed a healthy diet. Following a good diet is as difficult as any other aspect of preparation. It is our body's tendency to keep munching on something spicy or sweet in times of stress. Burgers, pizzas, chips, coke, chocolates become our go-to meals. On top of it, junk food is very addictive, and the more you eat, the more you crave it.

During the last year of my college, I realized that it was harmful in two ways. The obvious one is that we end up gaining weight, which in turn puts pressure on the neck and back, making it nearly impossible to sit for long.

Second, it takes a toll on our self-perception. Being in good shape makes us feel good.

But this in no way means you should stay hungry or divert your attention towards weight management. A few changes will serve the purpose. A diet rich in proteins, fruits, salads, daliya, dry fruits, curd, milk, green tea will keep your mind fresh and your body healthy. These choices become some of those 'extras' that might not seem to directly impact the output, but at the backend, they keep doing their work and ultimately lead to a great end result.

Since my parents were doctors, the importance of good diet was perhaps over emphasized. My father would keep my green tea, almonds, cashews, raisins and walnuts ready in the morning for me while my mother made sure to cut fresh fruits daily and cook daliya (porridge) for breakfast.

## Why jumping was my secret weapon

The other part of the healthy lifestyle is exercise. I feel that regular exercise is a must to sustain this long and difficult journey. I made it a point to give myself an adequate break after every sitting of study.

My favourite activity was to jump 200–300 times after every three hours of study. Jumping managed my back and neck pain, gave me satisfaction that my health was not being compromised and every time I exercised, the blood supply to my brain increased, improving my concentration power. I also felt it didn't take a lot of time and I could easily do this in my room without having to change clothes or go out.

When I had done enough work for the day, and could spare time for a long break, I would go for a 40-minute walk. Walking is one of those amazing exercises that serves multiple purposes. The obvious one is it keeps your muscles strong, saves you from becoming a couch potato and increases your blood circulation, which ultimately nourishes the mind.

But there's much more. It allows you to step away from your study and experience the world outside. You meet and greet people on your way, having been locked up by yourself in your room all day. An exchange of namaste with a broad smile is enough to make you feel connected and get a sense of belonging. On top of it, your self-image of being a nerd buried in the books all the time changes.

Walking also gives you time to connect with nature, which relaxes the mind and gives space to think clearly. Here I am referring to actual meaningful thinking. I used to find a lot of solutions to my problems while I was out for a walk. I am not the kind of person who could sit and meditate at one place – walking was my own alternative to relax both the mind and body.

If I walked with someone, I made it a point not to talk to them about my preparation. Rather I ensured we had funny or random conversations. If I walked alone, light music or a short audio story were my companions. Today when I look back, I can say it made a difference.

# 3

# How to Take Risks and Win

We often hear a lot of 'suno sabki, karo dil ki' (listen to all, but do as your mind decides) but implement only the first half. We 'listen to others', their experiences. When it comes to doing 'what we wish' and 'making a choice', we are afraid to take the less-travelled path.

The first major risk that I took in my professional life was during my college internship semester. We had multiple companies visiting the campus for internship recruitments, which ultimately gets converted to a full-time offer, your first-ever job. It was a big thing for all the students, especially for the computer science graduates, as many tech companies visited our college with hefty packages. So we, the computer science ones, were envied by students from the other departments with fewer options.

## When your options are limited, you really need to prepare

However, I was never enthused by the idea of making coding my profession. When the companies began to arrive, every computer science student, irrespective of their interests, started preparing enthusiastically for the interviews. I had to make a choice. On one hand, we had around 25-plus good software companies and on the other hand, two respectable non-tech companies, McKinsey and J.P. Morgan.

Since my second year, I had developed a desire to work at the finance company J.P. Morgan – part of it was also due to its location in Mumbai. I decided to take the chance and prepare just for the two non-tech companies.

McKinsey came on the second day of our recruitment – I sat for the entrance test, underprepared and lost my chance. I learnt yet another lesson of my life here. Never ever go without fully preparing, especially when the options are limited. I was overconfident and my lack of effort made me lose that chance.

So now a choice was to be made again. I could either wait for J.P. Morgan and skip all other coding jobs at MNCs like Amazon, Goldman, Sandisk and Cvent, or I could play it safe, change my game plan and try for the tech companies. I had a good academic record, a 9+

CGPA. So cracking the tech companies would not have been that tough had I made up my mind.

But I have always believed that doing anything half-heartedly doesn't materialize. So I listened to my inner voice and prepared for just one company, even though I knew it would visit after most other tech companies had come and gone. During that time, all my friends found placements and I felt intense pressure. Some of my peers mocked my overconfidence and, according to some, my stupidity.

Having lost my chance at McKinsey, my confidence was also a bit shaken. I could feel the burden of having nothing in hand if I didn't crack J.P. Morgan. 'What next?' was the question I had no clear answer to.

## There's only one way to make a risk payoff – work hard

Amid all this chaos, it was my family that came to my rescue. Given what a big deal it is for parents to see their children climbing up the career ladder with good jobs, the unconditional support of my mother and father came as a surprise to me. Their faith in my capabilities and my decision lifted my spirits. They told me not to think about anything but work as hard as I could to secure that internship.

I ensured that I did not leave any stone unturned. When you take unusual risks, you have to give 200 per cent to compensate. My close friends also helped me stay mentally strong. Some of them even helped to finalize my résumé the day before the submission. Eventually, I also made peace with myself and thought of a backup: preparing for the UPSC. So the plan was that if by chance I do not get this internship, I would accept it as destiny's call to start preparing for my childhood dream.

After a month-long preparation, the day arrived and with God's blessings, my hard work paid off and I got the offer from that one company I really wanted to join.

From then onwards, there was no looking back. I had realized the power of self-belief and the beauty of taking your own decisions, however absurd they may sound.

It was my first and the most important step towards taking risks.

I believe it is extremely important to take risks, and even more to work extra hard and maximize your chances. But making risky choices just to appear different or cool is stupidity.

In the process of proving something to others, you could lose everything, your self-confidence, your positivity, your belief in your capabilities and, of course, the recognition from others.

Hence, the 'why' behind every decision becomes very

important. There is absolutely no need to shout and tell everyone why you have made the decision, but internally you must be crystal clear about the reasons behind your choices.

Bagging my internship at the company of my choice was the most important step towards my journey of 'self-belief'. I had learnt that if I worked hard, I could convert that risk into opportunity and happiness would ultimately follow. This attitude was to determine my biggest decision, whether to pursue my childhood dream to be an IAS officer or go with the job offered at J.P. Morgan post the internship.

A lot of mental work went behind this decision, which I have dealt with in the next chapter.

# 4

# How I Decided I Would Do the UPSC

Often we are pushed into taking competitive exams because it's the 'right' thing to do. But is it the right thing for you? The journey is so hard. It takes a very long time, and the stakes are high. So, before you decide to sit for the exam, you should feel really sure you want to do this.

The conviction will also motivate you to work hard. I had always dreamt of taking the UPSC Civil Services Exam, but I made my decision slowly and cautiously after thinking through all aspects. This gave me a lot of courage to accept the consequences if things did not work out.

My UPSC journey started in the second year of college during the holidays. As I had decided not to apply to the tech companies, I had a lot of free time, which I wanted to utilize. So I decided to get an insight into the UPSC preparation.

Until that time, my dream of becoming an IAS officer was like a childhood fantasy. To get a clearer idea, I shifted to Patiala and started attending classes with a teacher who was very experienced in mentoring UPSC aspirants. I studied polity and economics there, my first-ever experience of a general studies subject.

Hard work never goes to waste. The conceptual clarity in economics I gained in Patiala helped me pass the J.P. Morgan finance interview in college. After bagging my internship, I did not continue with my UPSC preparation again. I wanted to first see how I felt about working in the corporate sector.

## A chance meeting

Two months before my internship, I had a chance meeting with the District Commissioner (DC) of Rupnagar (a district in Punjab). I had gone to the district for my driving test and had to do some paperwork near the DC's office.

I saw the DC's car outside the office and out of curiosity asked the guard if the DC was in her office. The guard, seeing my curiosity, suggested I go into the office and seek permission to meet her.

Meanwhile my mother had given up on me taking the driving test, seeing how adamant I was to meet the DC madam instead. But I had already made up my mind. I stood right outside the DC's office. The personal assistant asked me about the reason for the visit, and I very innocently shared my dream of becoming an IAS officer and said I wished to take her guidance. They brought a piece of paper to write the purpose of the visit and asked me to wait. After a short wait, I was called in. Even now, I remember every part of the conversation.

I told the DC that I had just landed an internship in an MNC and was confused about preparing for the civil services exam. She told me about the pros and cons of both worlds and asked me to introspect about what I wanted in life. She gave a sneak peek into her own lifestyle, how the initial years were to be spent working in rural areas, with no access to conveniences (like Swiggy, Uber, Dominos), which are undetachable parts of city life. But, she stated, the satisfaction one gets by contributing to positive changes at the grassroots level is immense. One thing that resonated with me was when she explained how happiness is a personal choice and cited examples of her friends from both the corporate sector and civil services who are unhappy and unsatisfied. She said, if given another chance, she would choose the same profession again.

That conversation had a deep impact on me. I understood that the decision to pursue the civil services preparation had to be solely mine and should be well thought out and not be based on wishful thinking. This helped me make my decision later on. The takeaway here is that you need to make full use of whatever opportunity comes your way. Had I prioritized my driving test that day over this sudden chance to meet the DC, I might not have been able to take this decision to pursue the services with so much clarity.

## Finally making up my mind

But I still hadn't fully made up my mind. I wanted to see the corporate world and the kind of opportunities it offered. I knew that before starting such a risky journey, I had to be totally sure. I had yet to discover what made me truly happy. The 'why' behind my decision had to be strong. So I decided to wait until I fully convinced myself.

Remember, the right time to start is when you are convinced and ready to make all the sacrifices that the journey will demand and not when others tell you to hurry before it is too late. If you start because of the fear of being left behind, you are most likely to be left behind.

An unsure fickle mind will always be confused, and mental confusion is not good, especially in such an uncertain, demanding choice.

When I went to Mumbai for my internship, I had a clear purpose – to study closely what the private sector had to offer and compare it with the public sector. And I did utilize those five months well. I talked to many people in the company – some seniors, some freshers, some super seniors from PEC – and had a sense of what my life could look like if I decided to pursue this line of profession further. I even had a word with a few other civil servants to get a deeper insight into their work, challenges and lifestyle.

I added one more hobby to my list that went a long way in helping me make the right decision. I started reading self-help books during my free time. I loved *The Monk Who Sold His Ferrari*. I began to visualize myself five years down the line and then 10 years down. For all those youngsters who have been asking me to help them, I am sorry to give you a disappointing answer – it's only 'you' and you alone who can and who should decide what's best for you.

## How to decide

Do your homework. Sit daily with a diary and a pen and note down your expectations and wants from life. Write down the options you have and the positives and negatives associated with each option. There is no perfect option. If you wish to enjoy the positives, you will have to bear the negatives too. But you can always choose the negatives that you are ready to accept. I personally feel that the positives in a career should not be the sole determinant of your decision; you should also embrace the negatives, those which you can live with.

If you feel that the challenges are insurmountable, it's better to drop the option because, with this mindset, even the positive aspects of the job will fail to satisfy you.

I took a good two and a half months to do this exercise, along with my internship work and weekend parties. I finally made up my mind halfway through my internship. The reason was that I knew the civil services would give me multiple opportunities to do good at the grassroots level of my country. In the corporate sector, I felt that the connection with society was missing and that I was not meant for those office cubicles.

I told my family about my ambitions, and they were totally supportive. Once I had made up my mind, the next question came: When do I start? I could have started immediately, but I wanted to 'enjoy to the fullest' before I entered this long, demanding journey. The next takeaway – there is absolutely no need to rush into things.

I made it a point to explore Mumbai, go for outings with my friends and to have fun, so that I had no regrets when I sacrificed all of this later. I knew that even if I were to get a pre-placement offer (PPO), I would not join. But I nonetheless made sure to give my best and try hard to get a PPO. It gives you a great psychological boost when you put your best into whatever work you are given. Mumbai was one of those experiences I will cherish all my life. I had my full quota of enjoyment and was ready to take the plunge towards my next journey. In fact, by the time I had packed my bags in Mumbai and reached Chandigarh airport, my mind was focused on the CSE. **You must fulfil the promises you make to yourself.** Ek baar commitment karli to roz roz apni bhi na suno. (Once you have committed to a decision, make sure to daily ignore the different voices in your head.) As soon as I landed at Chandigarh airport, I told my father to take me to the book depot to purchase the NCERT and other books.

This little step marked the beginning of the four-year-long journey!

# 5

# Handling the Pressure from Your Family

I have met so many parents who are keen to help their children and push them to dream big. But sometimes it takes the form of pressure, where you start feeling that it is mandatory to perform brilliantly or else you will let down the ones you love.

Their belief in you and their sacrifices make you feel guilty about not doing enough, which in turn, lowers your productivity.

Is there a way to deal with it??

I am afraid not!

There is a very thin line between motivation and pressure that our family and friends often overstep and we have to accept this. However, we can adopt two coping mechanisms:

## Understand and communicate

1. The first is to learn to empathize with them by stepping into their shoes and understanding that they are just trying to play their part well. Since they cannot help with the technical aspects, they want to participate in the journey enthusiastically as cheerleaders.
2. Second, when even this fails to pacify, you should politely confide your feelings in them. Communicate to them that their constant worry and expectations are taking a toll on your peace of mind. In my case, I wasn't always very polite! I would often get upset whenever my mother would ask about my score in the mock tests. But it's okay to tell them clearly what disturbs you.

## . . . but that's just 50 per cent

In my experience, both these approaches solve the problem by only 50 per cent. The other half can only be solved by your own mind. Remind yourself constantly that you are not obliged to fulfil anyone's expectations and are in no way the cause of their worries. You need to be practical and understand that you are responsible for your own fears and worries. You are not responsible for handling your parents' stress. However hard you may try, you cannot totally control the emotions of others. Let them do their karma (actions) and you do yours calmly. Be genuine with your efforts and make sure you are satisfied in your own mind.

The pressure ultimately comes from within and so must be mastered from within.

## How can your family play a positive role?

I write this chapter as a request to parents to wholeheartedly support their children who dream big. The family has an extremely important role to play in a journey like this. And by family, I also mean siblings. There are so many ways that families can help:

1. Supporting their children when they decide to take risks: What will our parents say? How will I convince them? What if they don't agree? These are some questions that plague us before we take a huge risk. Fear consumes a lot of mental space and deters many from pursuing their dreams. The moment our parents decide to stand by us in our choices, however tough they may be, we win half the battle. **Parents must realize that to achieve something bigger their child will have to leave something good.**

   I was very lucky as I didn't have to fight this battle. My parents backed my decision to leave a well-paying MNC job and start a new, risky, uncertain journey, keeping all their fears aside. But to get this kind of unconditional support, you will have to show them your conviction, determination and capacity to work extremely hard. Unless you respect your dreams, no one else will. Make sure your efforts reflect your aims. And you will no longer need to convince them. But there are some situations in which explaining your viewpoint to the elders becomes tricky. At those times, my brother came to my rescue. Your siblings can understand your viewpoints, your struggles much better as they would be closer to your age. My brother convinced my parents every time we had conflicting viewpoints. He would be the bridge between me and my parents. After my results, I got to know my parents and brother had a WhatsApp group regulated by my brother in which he even scolded them sometimes if they went overboard with worry and anxiety.

2. Protect yourself from undue societal pressure: We come under a lot of pressure from relatives, colleagues, neighbours and society. This pressure is, most of the time, routed through our parents. People tend to manipulate our parents and family members and force them to change our mind. You would hear all sorts of comments like: 'Bacchon mein toh bachpana hota hi hai, aapko samjhana chahiye'; 'MBA karwa dete, UPSC mein toh chances bahut kam hai'; 'Delhi kyun

nahi bheja bacche ko, ghar pe rehke kaunsi padhayi hoti hai'. (Children resort to immature behaviour, you must guide them; you could have guided them to take MBA, as there is very low chance of clearing the UPSC exam; why haven't you sent your child to Delhi – this kind of study is not possible in a home environment.) It is during these times that parents need to show grit and courage to ignore such comments and show confidence in their children's capabilities and their calculated decisions. My parents stood as a shield to protect me from such demotivating comments. Most of the time, I didn't even know what others were saying about my decisions. Everything was filtered, and only positive comments were allowed to reach me. My parents knew the importance of every minute and never asked me to accompany them to any social gatherings, functions or get-togethers and ignored all the conversations that my absence stimulated.

3. Supporting their mission as team members: Most of the time, our parents are ready to help us in our paths, but they don't know the ideal way. Thus, it becomes our responsibility to seek their help and convey to them how we need their time and efforts. I knew that my father was interested in general knowledge subjects and was fond of reading newspapers. So I requested him to study the UPSC CSE pattern and

help me with my current affairs preparation. He used to read newspapers daily and mark the relevant points for the Prelims and Mains. For the Interview stage, he read three newspapers (including a regional one). I would read the same newspaper the next day and his markings helped me in saving a lot of time and added extra points to my preparation that I could have missed due to paucity of time.

Similarly, I asked my brother to scan and upload my mock exam answer sheets on the web platform. It helped me save time.

He even helped me prepare for my CSAT exam and brush up on the subjects of my graduation course, Computer Science, for the interview. My mother, despite being a working woman, never let me do any household work. She would manage her professional work and all household tasks without disturbing my studies. Even during the COVID-19 pandemic, when she as a doctor had to play the additional role of a Covid warrior, putting in extra hours of work, and managing household chores since the domestic help could not come, she kept me out of all the worries at home.

My brother took on additional responsibilities like fetching groceries and helping my mother with household chores like washing utensils at certain times. They never complained. This is one support that I request all parents to extend to their girls because we in India mostly assume that daughters have an unsaid responsibility to contribute to household tasks, while the sons are given the freedom to spend their time however they want. We need to break these self-imposed norms and give girls time and space and support them in fulfilling their ambitions. My grandparents played their parts by praying for me every single day and soothing words by my grandma whenever I was tense added immense confidence.

4. Prioritizing their children's requirements: My parents knew that my only source of entertainment was sitting with them when they returned from their work and going for a walk with them. Since I was preparing at home, I didn't have many friends around and relied on family time to relax. So they made sure to be around during my breaks. They planned their work schedules according to my timetable. They would avoid attending functions, marriages, get-togethers and other such outings to be able to spend time with me.

5. Never compare your children with their friends: Parents unknowingly compare their children with their peers without realizing how it might impact them negatively. Instead, they must comfort their

children by telling them they have a unique store of talents and are different from others.

6. Emotionally support when one is going through a low phase: Parents are the first ones to know that their child is not doing well. And how they handle it makes a lot of difference. We need constant reminders that we are worthy of something good, that our efforts will pay off soon and that it's completely fine to face hurdles. And if it comes from our parents, it matters a lot. When your children fail, stand by them. Do not berate them, but help them figure out what went wrong, help them regain their confidence, and tell them that you are with them irrespective of the outcomes.

When the journey is long and arduous, many times you will feel like giving up. I remember in 2021, when the exam was postponed for the second time, I was tired and frustrated and felt like giving up. I felt as if I would not be able to sustain the journey anymore. At that time, my brother came to my rescue. He left important assignments at his workplace and instead spent his time listening to my fears, my struggles with boredom and encouraged me to start with the Mains preparation. I cannot imagine what would have been my fate if he had not been so generous with his time and company.

We also need a lot of mental support while waiting for the results. The thought 'what if we fail again?' doesn't let one sleep. I was very reassured by my parents that if I fail again, they will help me figure out what other options I can pursue. This kind of confidence helps one in dealing with the nervousness and anxiety that the time before the result brings.

7. Do not question their breaks: Parents should help their children come out of the guilt zone and encourage them to take good, productive breaks. Whenever I felt too tired after studying, my family was there to plan a perfect break; they would take me out for lunch or dinner or just for a stroll in the market and we made sure not to discuss anything related to the exam. My brother was my chill partner, and whenever I took a short break, we would go for a spin on the bike. I was never questioned when I decided to take a half or full-day break. The trust and faith my parents showed in me encouraged me to put in more effort and helped me stay on track.

There are so many other ways in which parents can help their children. Maintaining a positive atmosphere at home, motivating them every time their children feel it is impossible to get through, keeping aside their expectations and giving their children leeway to fly high in the open skies, to name a few.

Lastly, a small request for all the parents – please don't live out your ambitions through your children.

As an aspirant, the success you achieve finally is the result of the collective efforts of the entire family. You are the captain of the ship that cannot sail through without the help of other crew members.

## Friends

During my preparation, I have realized that it is not the number but the quality of friends you make that matters. It's extremely important to be in touch with positive friends who instil confidence in you. And even more important is to let go of those who always keep complaining. Beware of those who expect you to be part of every outing, every party to prove your friendship. They become burdens – they will always make you guilty of not doing enough to maintain the friendship. True friends will always understand the demands of your journey. They will not be jealous of your progress.

A friend who tells you to go back and study after an hour-long conversation is the one you should not let go of. But a point we often miss in friendship is that it is a two-way partnership. If you want them to respect your time, respect theirs. If you feel they are not always there for you, ask if you were. You cannot just expect and not deliver. Blaming them for not being there every time you need them, is over-demanding. As we grow up, we must become mature too. You might be going through a tough time, and your path might be riskier, but in no way does that give you the license to vent your frustration on your near and dear ones. It's this common mistake that makes us lose our beautiful relationships. Never belittle the problems of others. Never judge them if you don't want to be judged. And help whenever feasible. Be happy for their success and stand with them when they fail. Be apologetic when you cannot do so. You always get back what you give. I believe it's a misconception that you necessarily have to lose out on your good friends to achieve your higher ambitions. You only need to be genuine and communicate properly. So do not worry about losing your good friends on the path to your success because the genuine ones will anyway stay with you, come what may. I was in touch with a few college friends during my preparations and was lucky enough to have their support. They stood by me, encouraged me and always showed immense faith in my capabilities. At the same time, I distanced myself from a few who were negative and criticized me unnecessarily.

# 6

# I Just Can't Do It: Managing Stress

As I was appearing for an exam with a success rate of less than 0.1 per cent, this took a toll on my mental health. I was often anxious, fearful and doubtful. Especially on days when I scored low marks in mock papers or when I went blank while revising the topics I had covered earlier. It made me nervous and the feeling was just scary. I felt like I would never be able to cover the gap and my hard work was being wasted. I couldn't see any end to my struggles. It felt pathetic and I didn't feel like picking up my books again. It was during those days that the motto 'one step at a time' helped me regain my confidence and focus on giving my best at every step. When you know you have left no scope to push your limits further, it generates enough satisfaction, leaving no space for anything else.

But we do not have full control over our emotions,

especially the negative ones. Every time I used to hear someone making it in the fifth or sixth attempt, self-doubt would creep in. I would get tense and demotivated again. Fear of failing scares you like anything – your determination is put to test. On such days, you cannot allow your feelings to overpower you – you have to simply follow your schedule. I knew that if I waited for my motivation to be back, I would lose time.

So, on some days, you have to work mechanically, even if it is for the sake of following the timetable. Study even if half-heartedly, study even if self-doubt lingers, study even if it feels like fear will overpower you, study even if you just spent half an hour crying, but study you must!

That is why discipline becomes super important. It forms that impervious lining of your mental tank that does not allow your motivation to seep out.

## Don't wait for a good mood to start your studies

Going back to the 'why you started' is a good idea in theory but not always practical. Instead, say to yourself, 'I have to follow my timetable no matter what.' It's only a misconception that you can't study well when you are low. Ask yourself: 'Have I stopped eating and drinking while in a low mood?'

I faced this situation multiple times, and every time this

exercise came in handy. Once done with your study time, then get your dose of motivation during your breaks. Just push the demotivation to the back of your mind, study, complete your work and then bring it to the forefront and handle it. If you start paying attention to demotivation every time it creeps in, it will creep up on you again and again. After all, it's a good excuse for the mind to save itself from those hard hours of work.

Ghalib! Dil behlane ke liye khayal achha hai! (O Ghalib [to himself], this thought is apt to just pacify one's mind!)

## Ask the question 'why?'

Whenever I was low, I would vent my frustration and anger at my family on the pretext of minor things. They knew the phase I was going through and ignored or laughed at the minor pretexts I would use to show my irritation and would whisper to each other (Aaj bach ke raho, toofan aane wala hai! Pata nahi kis per aaj bijli giraegi!) (Oh! Beware! A thunderstorm is on its way. No one knows on whom the lightning will fall.) Their approach was to let me cool down and then lift my spirits by reminding me that I just had to concentrate on my efforts and not compare my journey to that of others.

I would always apologize after, and we would go to the park or a nearby cafe to cheer up.

If the demotivation is so strong that you feel like giving up altogether, then you need to go back to your 'why?', the reason you started the journey in the first place. Why did you choose to let go of all those good opportunities that came your way? What pushed you? What is at stake if you give up? Our mind needs these reminders. I always asked one question: *If not this, then what else?*

I knew I had no answer to the question as getting into administrative services was the only aim I had. And there was nothing else that would satisfy me. You just need to find your own needling questions that work for you to deflate the balloon of demotivation.

There will be times when even this won't work. For me, it was waiting for the results that was really tough. Even today, when I look back on that time, I get anxious. After the Prelims, the waiting period is approximately two weeks. But the good part is that you know that the preparation for the Mains has to start, irrespective of the results. What was extremely difficult to manage was the time after writing my Mains.

It was a good two months before the results were announced. And my mind was full of questions.

Should I study for the next Prelims?

Should I look for some other job as a backup?

Should I fill forms for other examinations, like the State Public Service Commission (PCS) Exam, the

Reserve Bank of India (RBI) Exam, the National Bank for Agriculture and Rural Development (NABARD) Exam and the Staff Selection Commission Combined Graduate Level (SSC CGL) Exam?

How do I pass the time?

If I do not study, will I lose touch with the subjects and have to start from scratch again?

These never-ending questions were slowly suffocating me from the inside.

I was tired of working so hard and wasn't prepared to start the journey again until I knew my mistakes or deficiencies. I wasn't able to enjoy my free time because I had not reached my destination yet. So here I was neither making the effort nor enjoying the rewards of my previous efforts. It made me guilty too for not being able to detach myself from the results, though I believed in 'karm karo per phal ki ichha mat karo!' (Do the action and don't cultivate desires for the result!)

As I had not filled out forms for any other exam, I didn't have anything else to prepare for.

And every day I tried to pass time talking to a friend or being with my family, an unwanted inferiority complex would grab me. I felt like everybody thinks of me as 'vehla' (an idle person with nothing substantial to do or a person whiling away the time). This complex was only in my mind; no one actually made me feel so. But you tend to assume so many things when things are not going well. Wanting to avoid that uneasy feeling, I tried finding my own nuskas (innovative solutions).

## How I calmed myself

I tried reading good books and watching some web series and new movies. I went for a short trip to Dharamshala with my college friends to get a whiff of the fresh mountain air and even attended a family function. Basically, I did things that I had avoided for three years. But to be honest, nothing could soothe my nerves fully. Some days, when I was surrounded by people, went by smoothly; it helped me step out of my overthinking zone for some time. The times when I sat in my room idle were the most difficult to pass. Each day seemed like a lifetime. At that moment, I was trying to prepare my mind for the possible failure that I might face and that made me miserable. The sheer thought of 'what if I fail?' haunted me.

The qualities that helped me withstand this pressure were patience and perseverance. It isn't as easy as it sounds. Patience is not only about waiting but having the ability to wait with a positive attitude. I tried to stay optimistic. You must radiate positive waves to get back positive results. Visualize yourself achieving success. It will help you stay calm and de-stress you.

Around one month later, I started preparing for the

Interview stage without obsessing over the results. In between, I planned some other hangouts with my friends and family.

Finally, the results were out – I had cleared the Mains exam. But after that it was again a good two months' worth of preparation for the interview.

That time was not smooth, either. Confusion reigned. My interview was on 12 May 2022, and the next Prelims examination was on 5 June 2022. *Should I focus only on the interview or also prepare for the Prelims in case I didn't clear the interview?* It was a question that kept lingering in the back of my mind every single day. Ultimately, I reached the conclusion that I couldn't face entering the same cycle again without knowing what went wrong. So I decided to concentrate on the interview and not prepare actively for the Prelims.

I decided that if I appear in the Prelims again, it would be a year later (2023), after a gap of one year. That would allow me to pause and think. Many experts say this isn't a good strategy – some panellists during the mock interviews also suggested that I keep studying for the Prelims.

I would feel stressed hearing these suggestions. It is really hard when you arrive at a decision and others make you doubt it. But I knew one thing: If I listened to others I would never be able to devote myself wholeheartedly to this lonely, long, uncertain journey.

My parents aligned with me and never forced me to do what I didn't feel like doing once I explained to them my thought process. But did I have the required backup or buffer? You will find out in the coming chapters.

## Handling criticism and others' opinions

When you are on a long and uncertain mission, criticisms will be regular, unwelcome guests. Random people will have thousands of arbitrary comments to make. Some will feel that you 'lack the so-called spark' or are not suitable enough or are over-ambitious, while others will mock your actions. Your efforts to steal a few minutes from here and there will be seen as 'egoism'. Your behaviour will be over-analysed by people so that they can give their expert opinions on whether you deserve to clear the exam or not. And when you fail, there will be people waiting to mock your efforts, ridicule you and prove that they were so right.

Now, it's up to you whether to react or respond. A wise person is one who knows that 'not every battle is worth fighting'. You need to make your choice: Waste your precious day crying over what others perceive of you, or be steadfast in your faith and work to reach your potential. Instead of nurturing hatred towards such people, feel sympathetic for them. Pray for them and move forward. There is no point in holding a grudge against someone and making it your purpose to prove things to them. It dilutes your real motive and unnecessarily sucks up your energy. Feeling hurt is natural, but allowing it to convert into simmering anger is a self-made, self-defeating choice.

I definitely felt bad when somebody made fun of my efforts, but the fact that their opinions did not determine whether I achieved my goal or not calmed me. Ignore and keep working, and your eventual success will speak volumes.

7

# How Important Are Backups?

Keeping a backup option is a wise strategy. When you know that you have another good career option waiting for you in case you fail, the journey feels a little less burdensome. The best backup when studying for the CSE is your undergraduate degree itself. Doing well academically and later securing a good internship in an MNC served two benefits: One, it boosted my self-confidence. I knew that if I put in my best efforts, I could get the best results. This attitude helped me in sustaining the UPSC CSE preparation too. Two, I was confident that in case I failed, I could return to these options anytime.

This is why it is advisable to pursue your graduation seriously.

## Backups mean you don't commit to your first option

I must admit that the option of returning to the corporate world scared me. I was fearful of going back to something I had consciously declined. Well-wishers suggested I should apply for other government exams as well, like the State PCS exams, NABARD exam, RBI exam and SSC CGL so that at least I would have a decent government job. But this made no sense to me. Why should I divert my focus towards something that I didn't want to do ultimately? And, that too, when I had not yet put wholehearted efforts into the actual CSE.

I went with my conviction and sat only for the CSE. During the first attempt, the pressure to sit for other exams was less. But when I failed, a few of my peers started mocking me and advised me to sit for other exams to secure my chances.

However, I was determined not to lose my focus and to work on my mistakes without any distractions. Even a minute dilution in your efforts can take you a step away from the destination. I felt it would be a waste of time filling the form for another exam, sparing a few hours daily to prepare for it, travelling to another city to write the exam and then waiting for the results.

## How no backup can become the backup

I was clear to not divert my attention away from my ultimate goal, and that too when I knew the reason behind my failure was a wrong strategy on my part. **It's your call at the end of the day, but I think that the CSE deserves two to three whole-hearted attempts without getting distracted.** I was even advised to sit for the CAT exam to secure a good college for an MBA. But I decided to skip it too. Having backups is essential, but you cannot just keep securing the backups without working hard towards the actual goal.

I have heard many aspirants claim, 'Chalo agar CSE nahi hua toh atleast koi aur exam nikal jaayega' (Oh! If I am unable to crack CSE, then at least I will be able to crack some other exam). This, my friends, is a wrong attitude. It's better to prepare for those 'aur/other exams' solely. At least you will spare yourself the hassle of standing on two stools. Some might feel my approach impractical as it 'puts all the eggs in one basket'. But this worked for me, **as sometimes having no extra backup pushes you to work even harder and not settle for less**. It's akin to the story of how, when pitted against a larger army, the commander of a smaller army ordered the burning of the ships upon landing on an isolated island. The smaller army emerged victorious – it was do-or-die for them. I understand that you need to secure your career when you fail multiple attempts, and it's fine to do that too. My only advice is: **Do not be extra cautious and start securing the backups before you have given your best to your actual goal**.

I've got a better backup for you while preparing for the CSE: **the habit of working hard, a focused mind, the right attitude and patience. If you honestly prepare for your Plan A, the learnings from it will automatically become your Plan B**. I knew I was putting in my best efforts and could observe the difference in me intellectually and personally. So even if I had failed, I would have utilized this knowledge to grab another opportunity that suited my interest. I could have gone for higher studies in sociology (my optional subject) and explored social entrepreneurship, or I would have joined an NGO. So this preparation in itself created so many new backups.

# 8

# How to Make Sacrifices

There is no such thing as a sacrifice – it's just a conscious choice you make to forego something good to get something better.

But it becomes tough when you know that you might lose both options – the good and the better – if you fail.

My journey towards making such choices started in 2018, in the final year of my college. That year, I went from being a socially active student to becoming a recluse, spending all my time in a single room with books, newspapers and self-notes all around.

## Want to succeed? Learn to enjoy your own company

I knew if I had to sustain this lonely journey, I needed to enjoy the company of my new companions, i.e., my books, notes and daily newspapers. In college, social life and coveted leadership positions mean a lot. But I mustered the courage and gave up my inclination for securing some coveted positions being offered in the college and the prestigious ones I was already holding. I felt that I had to learn to enjoy my own company and avoid being surrounded by a lot of people.

I didn't stay back for gossiping sessions after classes, avoided going to all lunch and dinner parties and made a new routine altogether, and it was during these days that walking in nature's lap became my most cherished hobby.

It did hurt initially to see some batchmates achieving everything that I had dreamt of. But it was just that I had redefined my dreams. It may sound a bit filmy but it is so true – kuch paane ke leeye, kuch khona padta hai (to attain something substantial, you must be ready to forgo something). I was lucky enough to have some of my friends by my side who helped me with the academic projects and excused me from get-togethers so that I could put in those extra hours of study.

## But did I miss the last year of fun completely?

Not at all. I used my breaks for some outings and made sure to fully enjoy the last two months of college and relish every moment with my friends. I was, in any case, not eligible to appear in the 2019 exam due to being underage, so I didn't lose too much on that front.

As I was not joining J.P. Morgan in Mumbai, I wanted to bid goodbye to the city that had helped me decide my goals. So, along with one of my best friends, I went on a short trip to Mumbai. It was my last trip – after that, the next three years until 2022, I had no time for holidays.

The mental preparation I did during my last year was of immense help in the journey. I had learnt to handle 'FOMO', the 'Fear Of Missing Out', well. I developed the habit of sitting for long hours and doing without movies, parties and holidays. I had figured out ways to spend my break time well (as outlined in the chapter on breaks in Part 2).

The choice was to get tougher in the coming weeks and months. For almost three years, 2019–2022, I did not attend a single family function, group video call with friends or watch movies in theatres (travelling to and fro wastes a lot of time and there is no option of speeding the video to 1.5x in a theatre) and avoided many get-togethers (except two or three). I would leave our dinner table discussions in the middle when my break time was over and wouldn't go for a walk until I completed the pre-decided amount of work.

## It won't feel like a sacrifice if you own your decision

I mostly avoided cribbing about missing out because I had the satisfaction that **I fully own my decisions** and I have never made any choice under pressure. So if you are on a journey just because your parents want you to do it, it's better to exit now. You cannot ever sustain anything forced upon you.

A humble note to parents: **The path to competitive exams is so hard. You might ensure that your child does not attend a party, but you can never ever make them study if it's not their choice.**

The feeling of having control over my own decisions energized and empowered me. Apart from these petty 'sacrifices', there were some hard choices that did make me guilty. When you are on a mission mode, you need to sacrifice spending time with your family, being part of the solutions to their problems, sometimes even ignoring whatever wrong is going on around you. It might make you feel self-centred, but that's essential.

You cannot allow yourself to be dragged into every family issue where your presence seems necessary. Things will eventually fall into place, but for you the time once gone will never come back again. So many times you will have to sacrifice a few of your responsibilities too. As mentioned earlier, during the pandemic, I felt guilty about not being able to help my mother with household chores. When my grandfather was hospitalized and the entire family was going through a very hard time, I couldn't always stand along with them and be their support system. You would really want to ensure your presence at some places but you will have to sacrifice those wants. You have to wisely differentiate – what is 'vital and essential' from what is 'desirable'.

So foregoing the satisfaction of supporting the family in everyday problems (whether emotional or financial support) is the actual sacrifice you make! This arduous journey requires such sacrifices.

## But I don't want to kid you – loneliness will be your companion

No matter how many friends you have or whether your family is by your side or not, the journey to the summit is always very narrow and lonely. It's hard for your friends to relate to this intense journey and even the most supportive family will not really be able to relate to it.

You neither have the time to talk openly nor the energy as you are already too tired of dealing with your inner fears, anxieties and fatigue. When you are too confused about your own emotions, it's next to impossible for others to get it and be your cure. A cocktail of feelings – nervousness, anxiety, fear, excitement – float around in your mind. The only thing to do is to remind yourself, 'It's just a difficult phase that shall pass soon.' There is not much you can do about this feeling.

As I said earlier, I made it a point to enjoy my loneliness, took it as a blessing to spend more time with myself and became my best friend. This loneliness helps you to grow personally. You learn to deal with your own problems, come to terms with your vulnerabilities, forgive yourself for the mistakes you have committed and make peace with your failures.

Today I miss this 'me time'. So the next time you feel lonely, remember that it's not abnormal to feel that way, and anyone who has completed the journey has passed through the same phase. Instead, try to utilize the loneliness by giving yourself a dose of positive self-talk discussed in the upcoming chapters.

# 9

# Guilt

We tend to be guilty about every other thing. When I was preparing for UPSC CSE, guilt always took a toll on me. The guilt of not being able to study enough, the guilt of taking frequent or long breaks, the guilt of wasting a lot of time overthinking, the guilt of not being able to help in family matters and the guilt of feeling guilty itself.

We spend so much time feeling guilty that we don't realize that it saps our productivity.

## How I dealt with guilt

How did I deal with it? It was extremely difficult to get rid of overthinking, I must admit. It was tough to bring my mind back to my mission when it crossed many stages of imagination. But you must put a full stop to these thoughts to be able to concentrate on genuinely important things. I made a simple rule for handling guilt. Whenever I felt guilty about something, I analysed if it was justified or not.

What is unjustified guilt?
Guilt that you can't do anything about is unjustified guilt. If you start paying attention to it, you will compromise on your end goal. Whenever I felt guilty about not being able to talk to my friends during their lows or when I left in the middle of a serious discussion at home, I knew this guilt was unjustified. Because if I had decided otherwise, I wouldn't have achieved my big dream. Do not fall into this guilt trap, as it compromises your end goal.

A rule that no one talks about, and which to my mind is inevitable, is 'prioritizing yourself and your dreams'. There is a stark difference between selfishness and self-priority. The latter is vital if you want to achieve success. You need to respect your dreams, your aims and your time first, only then will others respect it. Many aspirants feel difficulty in managing their personal relations along with their aims.

## Prioritize yourself

My advice is, to achieve your goals, communicate your priorities very clearly first to yourself, then to your close friends and family members. You cannot be emotionally weak if you want to sail through your journey victoriously.

You ought to choose yourself and your time over the demands of others. Nobody else will tell you to do so.

There is a reason that such journeys take a lot of mental grit, strength and toughness. You need to be extremely strong and resist all unsaid pressures. Take it this way: your genuine well-wishers will definitely understand the demands of your journey. And the day you achieve your dreams, their happiness will compensate for all the times you were absent. But if you miss your chance, you will regret it your entire life. And your regret and sorrow will invite misery for your loved ones for whose happiness you compromised with your dreams. So it's a lose-lose game.

Sometimes, when you know you are not doing enough, it makes you feel guilty. And that guilt is justified. It encourages you to work harder and invest more time and energy in getting closer to your goal. Take that guilt as a stepping stone. And aim to get rid of it as soon as possible, in a mission mode.

## 10

# Change the Way You Talk to Yourself

No matter what you are going through, you have one person who knows everything that is going on inside you and has all the solutions to your problems. That person is YOU. Befriend yourself, enjoy your own company and embrace the companionship of loneliness. Master your mind before it masters you.

Remember – your mind manifests what you first visualize on your mental screen. In your free time, appreciate your efforts, pat yourself on the back, calm your fears and send the right messages to your mind. Choose to say again and again, 'I am blessed as I am doing well and will do better' and avoid saying, 'I am a failure, I cannot do anything.'

## The right message

You might not be convinced that such an unconnected thing has to do anything with your success.

Isn't the hard work you put in enough to determine your results? You are partially right, as **the right kind of messaging to yourself is essential to complete the package**. It is here that the re-enforcing power of your subconscious mind comes into the picture. Being the biggest beneficiary of positive self-talk, I cannot resist giving it enough credit. My father would reinforce this point every time I would come downstairs after studying and begin to rant about how I was not giving my best or how I was afraid that I would fail. He reminded me to choose my words carefully as words are the triggers for ensuing thoughts and actions.

My father would instead push me to say, '**I have been doing well and will surely do better**' and '**God is going to help me if I help myself.**' Even my grandfather was extremely particular about it. Sometimes, when you have people around correcting you every single time you speak negatively about yourself, you tend to feel frustrated. All I wanted to do was vent my frustration and exhaustion, and all I got was a pep talk! It made me even more irritated at times. My father would assertively tell me how I was inviting failures with this negative self-talk. He reiterated that **those who fully believe in their own selves and are grateful are unstoppable in the pursuit of their goals**. Had he not been particular about it, I wouldn't have been writing this chapter and telling you all how much of a difference it makes. Unfortunately, I learnt this lesson a little late after faltering in the first attempt. While preparing for my first CSE attempt, I used to be extra harsh on myself, feeling unnecessarily guilty about taking breaks or never satisfied with my efforts. I believed it was important to tell my mind that 'I was not putting in my best', but this had a negative impact on my self-perception and confidence.

Thanks to constant nudging and reiterations by my family, during my second attempt I finally developed the habit of sending the right messages to my mind. I started choosing words like 'will' over 'should', 'possible' over 'impossible', 'can' over 'cannot' and actually felt energetic, confident and in control of things. I visualized myself succeeding in this attempt and even wrote on my whiteboard: 'I will be in the Top 10.'

## How positive self-talk helped me

My habit of positive self-talk really helped me through one crisis while I took my exams. In the five-day break after writing the five GS papers, my health deteriorated.

I came down with a severe cold, and it took a turn for the worse, with me developing a serious gut infection the day before the optional exam. I had not eaten anything and was surviving only on nimbu paani (lemon water) for two days.

Anyone preparing for the CSE will know the importance of the optional paper. I knew it was a 'do-or-die' situation. But I was extremely low on energy. A day before the sociology exam, I was trying to remember a few theories of the important thinkers and I went blank.

The fear of failing at the very final stage was taking a toll on me. The day before the exam, I shut my eyes and just repeated to myself in a loop, '**I will be able to give my best tomorrow, and what will determine the results is the actual work I have done all these years, not the revisions skipped the day before**.'

In the middle of the exam, I felt dizzy and lost. I took a deep breath and recalled, 'Your mind will believe and respond to what you tell it repeatedly.' So, I said to myself, '**I can do it.**' I credit my success to this self-talk because if I had given up mentally, I am sure I would not have made it. I felt so ill and stressed that when I came out of the hall and read the question paper again, I could not recall a single thing I had written.

Today whenever someone asks me if I had expected this rank, my response is, 'I didn't know what to expect.'

You can only expect this when you evaluate your performance. I knew I had done well enough in GS, but with sociology, I had no way of knowing. I just knew that I had done whatever was best possible in those circumstances. Finally, my 287 marks (among the highest this year) came as a beautiful surprise.

## Training your mind

Self-talk also helps you embrace the loneliness of this kind of journey. So the ultimate message is to utilize your alone time to train your mind so that it listens to you. It might be about waking up early, avoiding the temptation to watch a new movie or skipping a day of study. You can always ensure that apart from your intellectual growth, you utilize the time to grow personally by cultivating lifelong good habits.

Be sure not to run away from your fears and negative thoughts. Make it a point to tackle them head-on. Remember the old saying: **Tough times never last, but tough people do**! I visualized that I would emerge victorious and constantly reminded myself of it whenever self-doubt crept in.

The problem with most people is that they run away from themselves. Or when they don't, they tend to feed their minds with negative thoughts. It is a natural tendency of the mind to think about all the 'bad' that can happen to us, and no wonder it is a vicious downward spiral cycle. It is up to us to divert our mind to wherever we want to take it rather than falling into the trap.

## 11

# When Everything Is Planned, Where Does Uniqueness Fit?

There are a lot of rules to be followed in acing the competitive games. So where does this leave your individual style? Should you give up your approach and blindly listen to the videos, the coaches, the toppers and your peers?

During any journey, you will meet a lot of people who will try to influence you in one way or the other, making it seem as if it is only their advice that will determine your success. It takes courage to avoid all those influencers and shut the background noise to keep doing what you feel is right.

### How I made my own rules

I used to hear a lot about toppers utilizing group study as a mode of preparation, joining multiple Telegram groups to stay connected with fellow aspirants and getting their answers checked by peers. But I was not willing to do any of these.

I was a self-study person. I knew that I needed time with myself to grasp concepts. I did not even allow someone to sit in the same room (even if they promised to stay quiet). So there was little chance of feeling comfortable with group study. This was also one of the reasons I didn't go to Delhi. I was not a coaching class type or someone who will be able to study in a library. I needed my own space to study well.

I was told many times to get in touch with other aspirants. I tried it a couple of times only to realize that this was not something that brought out the best in me. Rather, I felt guilty about wasting time.

The point I am making is that **you should follow others' strategies only as far as the 'what to do' is concerned and leave the 'how to do it' to yourself.** There is no one rule here.

**The main aim is to get your work done; the place, time and manner do not matter.**

Similarly, don't let others decide when is the best time for you to take time off. You are your best judge. **As long as you are honest with yourself**, you need not justify your actions to anyone else.

I remember watching the web series *Mumbai Diaries* a

month before my Prelims exam. I did not regret it because I was not giving in to my mind's desires, but rather it was a conscious decision as I badly needed a break to put in my best efforts in the last month. In case your peers pressurize you to push yourself a little in the end when you know there is not enough energy left, do not succumb to the pressure. Do not argue either, but make that call. Watching the web series did help. The last month went pretty smoothly with less cribbing and more productivity.

The other dilemma of aspirants is whether to make handwritten notes or online notes on a notepad. Again decide as per your comfort. Whenever I would hear someone telling how they saved a lot of time by making online notes, I would feel unsure as I have always felt more comfortable with pen and paper. So I decided to do what makes me feel more satisfied and productive.

When I started preparing formally in 2019 after graduation, I joined a coaching class in Patiala that commenced at 5.30 a.m. In those sessions, our teacher would lecture at great speed and we had to understand, process, write and repeat.

My hands would ache, and my fingers began to swell. But by the time I stopped attending the classes, I had developed a habit of writing very fast. I kept that habit alive and made handwritten notes throughout my preparation.

This practice helped me in two ways. One, I could adapt myself to write the three-hour long paper within the time frame, which is extremely crucial. Second, I was able to absorb the content faster. When you write, your mind automatically creates visuals that get stored in your brain's hard disk and are much easier to retrieve later on. I was able to memorize the content faster and needed fewer revisions.

I even clubbed my note-making with my answer-writing practice, which was like killing two birds with one stone. My notes were structured and written as an answer should be. So this is another place where I created my own approach as per my preference.

You should not start taking handwritten notes just because I did. Do what works for you. One last example – I was not the person who could prepare well from others' notes. Of course, I referred to a few of them to get the gist of what is important, but I never relied on them as my basic material. I just did not feel that connection.

When you make your notes, it is never to explain concepts to others. While making my notes, I skipped so many points that I felt needed no writing or that were well ingrained in my mind. That's one reason it felt so odd when I received so many messages requesting my notes.

On the other hand, I know of a few fellow officers who secured good ranks consulting the notes of others since they never felt comfortable making their own notes. So next time when self-doubt creeps in and you find it difficult to follow the techniques of others, just go with your strengths and devise your own techniques. **Everyone is gifted, but most people never open the package**.

Trust your sixth sense and go for it.

## 12

# How Important Is It to Plan Well and Stay Consistent?

My end goal was to pass the exam. Your end goal could be anything – starting a company, securing a good job in an MNC or becoming a doctor. But you can't just rely on that broad goal to keep yourself on the right track. You need to break it into components, which will differ according to each person's goal. In my case, the components meant subjects or topics I had to complete studying for the exam. To fulfil each component, I broke down my tasks into multiple plans – a broad yearly plan, a three-month plan, a monthly plan and a weekly and daily plan.

Proper planning is extremely crucial. An enthusiastic beginning without a proper layout is most likely to get you off track. In 2019, when I started preparing for my first attempt, I went with the flow. I thought things would fall into place on their own. But they never did. Despite getting four extra months due to postponement, I could not revise my syllabus well because of my lack of planning. It only works well in the movies when they say 'go with the flow'.

## How to make your plan

Making a plan is like making a broad timetable on the content/subjects to be covered in a particular time frame. Say you want to get done with your first reading of all the subjects in six months, then keep a dedicated slot for each subject and follow it religiously. The focus has to be on following those plans to the best of your capacity, even if it means devoting extra time to the areas you feel you are weak.

Make the best use of that every single day and do each topic with the same zeal and enthusiasm – this is what we mean by consistency – the word you would have heard in every topper's interview.

It is much easier said than done. We unknowingly tend to bypass some components, calling them boring or irrelevant for the exam. Sometimes, while reading the topics that were tough to memorize, like article numbers in polity or about a species in a national park in environment, I tried to bypass these by assuming the paper may not have questions from these portions. Or even if there were, they would be not more than one or two. I also observed many fellow aspirants compromising on some subjects like ancient and medieval history either because they were tough to remember and required extra time, or due to the misconception that the questions would be asked outside the book. I did that during my first attempt only to realize that all the subject areas I had left out were dominating the exam. In an exam as competitive as the UPSC, every question counts and you can never predict what will be deemed important by the examiner. In one year, polity may dominate the paper and in another year, it may be economics or history. You cannot take any chances here.

## What I mean by consistency

This is where I misunderstood consistency as only in terms of putting the same amount of time daily. But it means putting the same effort and enthusiasm into every component (in my case, the topics and subjects) also. If by devoting maximum time to my favourite subject I am able to solve 90 per cent of the questions from it in the exam but fail miserably to get even 50 per cent right in another subject, I am still losing. It's as simple as that. If you dilute anywhere, it gets reflected in the results.

In my second attempt, I made sure to give fairly equal weightage to all subjects, and my hard work was rewarded. I got two extra questions correct in ancient history as I had read the NCERT textbooks thoroughly.

One cannot compromise on any parameter. We often do that and cheat ourselves by claiming that we have worked really hard. But ultimately, it is these ignored components that turn the tables against us. In my first attempt, I gave a wrong sense of security to myself that I had completed the subject even when some 'seemingly unimportant' portions were left out by me.

In addition, to be truly consistent, the work towards the goal has to be done daily, putting in the same hours every single day. The key to getting through is not putting in five hours in one day and 15 hours the next day, assuming that would make up for the less time spent the first day. You have to follow a routine and there is no space for boredom or a 'chalta hai' (it shall be okay) attitude here. Following your schedule properly each day is calming and generates satisfaction. I actually started enjoying having a routine.

Remember, you are competing with lakhs of aspirants – the best of them will be very driven, consistent and thorough.

I have discussed in Part 2 what my timetable looked like, how I segregated my broad goal into short-term targets, what went wrong with my planning in the first try and the corrections I made in my subsequent attempt.

## 13

# Happiness – An Important Accompaniment for Struggle

I have often noticed there exists a myth that one can be happy only when one's goal is achieved. We hold back our joy as if it's some limited feeling, which if experienced now, will be exhausted when the result is in. Even society lives with the misconception that a focused individual ought to be serious. We automatically associate that nerdy, unsatisfied look with a studious child. It is similar to the perception that you are intelligent if you wear spectacles. No wonder zero number specs seem to be in trend.

Such unhealthy messages get so imprinted in our minds that we assume we deserve happiness only when we achieve our aim. In our country, there is another reason to not showcase your joy – 'kahin nazar na lag jaye' (lest somebody casts an evil eye). But let me tell you, this is the biggest injustice we do to ourselves.

Being serious about your aim doesn't mean that you have to start avoiding happiness and carry a worried look everywhere you go. You not only punish yourself but also your family and friends who are so fed up tolerating that 'always sad, grieving, disappointed face' of yours. No one likes to be around an unhappy, unsatisfied person. Ask yourself. Would you ever want to spend your time with a person who is always cribbing or has reasons to be unhappy?

## My mantra

My mantra during the preparation was to try my best to be happy about the efforts that I was putting in. An unhappy mind does not let you focus. The mind runs after instant gratification and if you don't allow it, it keeps you demotivated and unenthusiastic until you feed it with good positive thoughts. By being happy about your efforts and rewarding yourself every day, you begin to enjoy the process. It is unbelievable how a number of persons find happiness evading them when it is the most easy thing. Reflect on your journey and analyse whether your productive days were the ones when you were happy or grave.

But I know the trouble starts with the question, 'What should I be happy about?' We are still struggling to become something, to reach our destination, to feel worthwhile. Amid all this, what is there to be happy about?

Well, **the efforts you put in daily as per your planning should become the reason for your happiness**. When you stop waiting for the final results and start enjoying your daily efforts, you will not feel burdened by your goal. Fulfilling your daily targets and what you have decided for the day will become your only driving force because your mind will crave that happiness and satisfaction. Be happy about small achievements.

## Replace tension with cheerfulness

During my second attempt, I replaced 'tension' with 'cheerfulness'. Whenever I ticked a date on my calendar, indicating I had done my best for the day, I would celebrate before bed and pat myself on the back. My mind started craving this satisfied feeling, pushing me harder every passing day to tick the calendar. I allowed myself to laugh at myself, have fun and be happy with the present. I observed that I started feeling lighter and my study was no longer a burden. This was my mantra to stay motivated every day by reminding myself of the positive feeling my efforts would give me when the day ended instead of worrying about the result.

That did not mean I was never sad or never felt discouraged, or that I had some button to automatically switch on the happy mode. Some days were really bad. I felt miserable and not worthy, especially when I could not complete my daily targets, got poor marks in my test papers or could not complete them on time. However, every time I couldn't achieve my targets, I made sure to analyse the reason behind it and then root out the problems. If you get fewer marks in a paper, revise harder and take more mock papers. These extra efforts will automatically bring back your happiness.

I clearly remember one such incident. It was the evening after my Prelims 2021. I compared my answers with some answer keys to guess my chances. I was extremely disappointed and disheartened, for it seemed my chance of making it to the list was negligible. I spent the entire night crying – yes, literally! But I woke up in the morning and decided to celebrate my efforts. I knew that irrespective of the result, I would not get those days back when my mind was free after an exam gets over. If by chance I cleared it, I would have to resume my preparation. Even if I did not, the path was going to be tough. So, I got a grip on myself and enjoyed myself to the fullest. I went for a walk to Sukhna Lake in Chandigarh with my father and brother, hopped between multiple cafes, ate my favourite dishes, met my friends, gossiped and even had a sleepover at my best friend's place.

The next morning, the routine continued. I was not thinking much about the results because I knew I could not do anything about it. But a happy and satisfied mind invites happiness, and on my way back home from Chandigarh, I got a call from my mother and brother telling me that as per the new answer keys, I had a chance to clear the Prelims. And yes! I did clear it. When I look back, the decision to utilize those two days happily played a crucial role. I was ready for the next innings, to work even harder for the Mains.

# 14

# Have a 'No Excuses' Policy

Another mantra that helped me sail through this tumultuous journey was a 'no excuses' policy. You cannot let any factor become an excuse for not doing your karma. It was a non-negotiable policy followed in our home. Remember the other one – the 'positive self-talk'?

**Every issue is only as big as we make it**

Every time I cribbed about not being able to study due to either some noise nearby or a body ache, I was politely told by every single person in my home to not come up with excuses. I would go to all three of them separately (my mother, father and brother), complaining about the same incident, hoping one of them would let me off the hook and show me some sympathy. But they only had one response. Let's find the possible solutions. Do not just focus on the problem. Go to another part of the house if the noise is a distraction, or take medicine if you are not feeling well.

I knew they were right. We just do not want to accept that we are being lazy or irresponsible – and it is irresponsible not to find solutions.

Every issue is only as big as we make it. The moment someone makes you realize that you are using it as an excuse to avoid work, you feel like hitting something hard. But after that moment of irritation, I did recognize that I was being irresponsible and an escapist.

So next time, before blaming the cold winters for not being able to study, or your bad PG food, or a dull stomach ache, or an altercation with a friend or any xyz reason, please keep in mind that it does not matter. Ultimately, you are going to pay for it, you are going to suffer, and in case you are preparing for the CSE, UPSC is not going to be extra kind to you for experiencing all these miseries.

## How I learnt this lesson

I didn't learn this lesson easily. It took me a long time, until after I had failed in my first attempt. Just a month before my first Prelims in 2020, my father was posted to the Dedicated Covid Centre (DCC) on duty, and he was away from home for two weeks.

I was extremely disturbed as we had seen so many doctors succumbing to COVID-19 while on duty, and it started affecting my performance in the last crucial days. I wasn't able to concentrate fully and kept blaming the situation.

Once walking back from my class, someone on a motorbike snatched my phone from my hand even as I was using it. I unnecessarily wasted so many days overthinking the incident and then made it an excuse for not studying well. Yes, it is natural for someone to get disturbed by such an accident, but if I were the kind of person I later became for my second attempt, I would not have compromised on my studies for such reasons.

**Ultimately each and everything counts. Come what may, you cannot compromise on your work**

Don't get me wrong – it wasn't as if I was undisciplined during my first attempt. Many of you reading this book will pride yourself on your discipline too. I was extremely diligent about some aspects like attending every class at 5.30 a.m., irrespective of the weather conditions or my body longing to get a little more sleep. In December, I would walk to my classes in the moonlight. Not a single person was on the roads because of dense fog.

Where I faltered was that I was yet to make 'no excuses' a habit, and unless you follow this policy consistently every time, it does not yield results. After I failed my first attempt, I managed to ingrain this habit through intense retrospection and analysis.

## What 'no excuses' is not

Let me clarify what the 'no excuses' policy is *not*. It's not about ignoring the problems that come your way. It's not even about suddenly becoming a superhero who stays unaffected by whatever happens around. It's about not ranting and blaming the problems for your failures. It's about the need to look at alternatives with an open, clear mind. The issue arises when we make the issue unconquerable and merely keep lowering our productivity.

Even successful people have fear, doubts and worries. They just don't let these feelings stop them. I always remembered the profound guiding prayer: '**God grant me the serenity to accept the things I can't change, the courage to change the things I can and the wisdom to know the difference.**'

Here are a few problems I faced, which were earlier excuses. But I learnt to manage them by looking for solutions:

I always prepared for current affairs by perusing daily news analysis on websites. I would download the PDF, mark the points and save it. But during my first Prelims preparation, I ended up not revising them because it was difficult to read so much on the laptop. I did not get the printouts thinking that would involve too much paper and make a mess. It was totally an excuse to avoid that extra hard work.

In my next attempt, I tried to focus on the alternatives. We got a printer at home, and I started taking printouts daily. We knew this would be a fruitful investment, although it was costly. But knowing when to use our money and for what purpose is also a calculated act of wisdom; something I realized slowly.

This time I made sure that the bulkiness of the material was not an excuse, and I revised the marked portions of each and every daily analysis, date-wise, before the exam. Yes, it was tiresome and consumed time, but then there is no substitute for hard work. I realize affordability maybe an issue in such circumstances, so I am not propagating this as the only solution. The point is to rise above 'cursing the situation' and look for genuine ways out. I found mine this way. You could even think of something better. But THINK you must!

Another incident from the winter of 2021 comes to mind. After I had cleared the Prelims, I would sit on the terrace in the sunlight and study there. It has been a favourite spot of mine since my college days.

Right after my Prelims, the construction of two new houses started just opposite my house. I could not concentrate properly, with the noise of hammers and bricks and workers gossiping. More worrying was that the new buildings obstructed sunlight. From the direction of the balcony near my room, a neighbour's TV blared. I tried a lot to adjust but I could sense that my work was getting compromised.

I sat inside my room for a few days. We requested the workers not to play loud music, and they were kind enough to oblige. So one part of the problem was solved. But the major one remained: Where could I study and get good sunlight too?

My brother and I brainstormed and found only one solution. On our terrace, we had a store room that opened to the opposite side (away from the construction noise), but the wall of the store room obstructed the sun. Our idea was to get that wall demolished. We knew it might not be easily acceptable to our parents, as it involved a lot of hassle and we had to see if it was safe for the building.

I still remember that discussion at our table. It took some time for my mother and father to realize that we weren't joking. After all, it isn't every day that your children ask to permanently demolish a part of your house to create an ideal space for studying for an exam, that too when the preparation involves just two months. But to my disbelief, my parents agreed the moment they understood how important it was for me.

Within two days, my mother emptied the store, workers were called by my father to demolish the wall, and I studied happily ever after.

**The key takeaway is that we have to be practical and understand that however hard we try, we cannot change others or blame our situation for everything wrong happening to us.** We have to make a choice – to hold on to our excuses and pacify our minds or to solve them in the best way possible.

# 15

# Dealing with Tragedies beyond Your Control

I can neither tell you the ideal way to deal with tragedies nor claim that what I did was the best and should be replicated. I can only share my experience of what I felt and how I overcame it. I got immense help from some examples of earlier aspirants who had gone through such situations and so want to share mine too. This is the only chapter I wished I didn't have to write. This is the only experience I regret having to go through in my entire journey. But one has to bow before things that are not in one's control and still stand strong.

**Some heartbreaking news**

Four weeks before my Mains exam, we had a heartbreaking incident in our family. My grandfather, who was eagerly waiting for me to write my exam and visit him after that, was suddenly hospitalized due to breathing issues. His oxygen level had dropped to SPO2-60 per cent (normally above 90 per cent).

My father rushed to Sunam, a small town in Punjab, our native place. Grandpa's condition became serious, and he was shifted to a bigger hospital in Patiala. Since childhood, our grandpa had been my brother Tushar's and my friend guide, Santa and our go-to person whenever we felt low. We had learnt our basic morals and values from him. And visiting our grandparents on vacations was something we waited for the entire year. He had stood by me throughout like a strong pillar. His daily prayers for both me and Tushar imbibed positive energy in us. I was waiting for my Mains exam to get over and spend plenty of time compensating for the last few years. But the day I came to know about his hospitalization, my world shattered.

He had been in very good health so this came as a sudden shock. My father went to Patiala to be beside him, but he was adamant that we stay put.

I was afraid of losing my grandfather, feeling guilty that I had not been able to spend enough time with him due to my preparation. I even started cursing myself for not clearing the exam on the first attempt! Amid all this chaos, there was an extremely negative feeling at the back of my mind, the guilt of not being able to study for my Mains examination. I went through the typical emotions you go through in such a state – when you cannot do as expected, you feel like you are losing on every front and you want to shout 'Why me?' but get no answers. I had never felt more frustrated with my preparation than on those days. I just wanted to be excused from writing the exam. But eventually, I got a grip on myself. I was running behind the schedule of my Mains test series and was only able to revise a few of my handwritten notes. My loss of momentum just 30 days before the Mains began to stress me out.

## Breaking down

Grandpa's condition was deteriorating and he was shifted to the ICU. That was the point I completely broke down. My pillars of support – my father, my brother, my mother, my grandma – themselves needed support. It was at this time my mother came to my rescue. They say mothers know when their child needs what. She had somehow judged that I was falling apart and read my mind. I do not know how mothers do this each time. She knew that I really wished to meet grandpa once but couldn't say it for fear of being declined.

My mother made the decision and asked me to

accompany her to the hospital the next day. I could meet my grandpa for about 15 minutes only. He was upset to see me wasting my time during this crucial phase of my studies.

Even though he was struggling with a BiPap machine (a type of ventilator with a face mask, a nasal mask and nasal plugs attached to it), he kept smiling. His focus was on uplifting my spirits and he encouraged me to stop worrying about his health and just concentrate on my preparation. He even ordered me not to visit him again in the hospital. I had no idea that this meeting with my grandpa was my last ever with him.

A few days later, the doctors asked us to shift him out of ICU so that he could spend his last days with his family. My deepest fear was suddenly coming to reality and I was unable to do anything. I would keep crying most of the day, trying hard to divert my mind to studies.

I wanted to spend the last few days with my grandpa. I was super angry with my parents for not allowing me to do that. Now when I look back, I cannot even imagine how hard it was for my parents to make that decision and to prioritize my dreams and ambition over my stubbornness. They were fighting two hard battles. My mother contacted one of my best friends and a few other well-wishers to help me through all this. I learnt my hardest lessons during that time. We cannot do anything about things not in our control, but we can and should do our best in the things under our control.

I decided to do my karma, which was to give my best to my studies and be in touch with my grandpa through video calls. During the next two days, I relied upon my 'no excuse' policy and tried to find ways in which my mind could return to my studies properly.

## How I turned myself around

I started solving the three-hour test papers. I thought this might help get me back to the flow. To my amazement, whenever I started writing the paper, I forgot everything and was totally engrossed in the exam. My only aim was to complete the paper on time, and this rush against time was helping me focus.

With this mock solving, I began to slowly come back on track again. In retrospect, this practice through mocks became my secret to success. The other thing that came to my rescue was my prior work. I was ready with the raw material as my notes were already made before the Prelims exam, and I had even written a few mocks before. (I discuss my plan in detail in Part 2.)

**So another lesson I learnt is never to leave things to the last moment. You can never predict the circumstances in the future.** Had I left any major portions during these few months before my Mains, I am sure I wouldn't have been able to crack the exam.

One more personal lesson I learnt during this time was by looking at my father's conduct. He was staying day and night at the hospital with my grandpa and was finding every way he could to give him a few more days and hours of his life. Being a doctor himself, he would go through all the reports consult specialists from other hospitals, and barely sleep for days. I felt tense, sympathetic and proud at the same time.

My grandpa could sense the irreversible damage to his lungs and consoled the family members not to feel disappointed. He was more than satisfied with the efforts made and was ready to gracefully depart. And witnessing him and my father play their parts so strongly, I was pushed to play my part of the assigned karma strongly. And I did maintain that grit.

## Grieving but not letting it get me down

On the morning of 13 December, I got the news of my grandpa's demise. It was devastating but I had learnt to become mentally stronger through the pain of acceptance. This time it was not uncontrollably distressing when I took the decision to not attend the last rites. I knew that was what my grandpa would have wanted.

I was alone at home for the next few days. I could not keep my mind off it. But I was determined not to waste this time. I decided to solve mock papers, attempting one full paper in the first half (9.30 a.m. to 12.30 p.m.) and the next from 2.30 to 5.30 p.m.

And then I put in at least three to four hours revising the notes and material. My day was made up of studying, crying and studying again. Grieving is a natural emotion, but I had, with time, learnt the art of combining it with some serious work. By this time, only three weeks were left for the Mains. I worked really hard to compensate for the lost time.

The distractions existed both mentally and physically with frequent visitors coming home to offer their condolences. But I made it a point to spend most of the time in my room and avoid interactions. I did a lot of positive self-talk and took solace in music (even recording a few songs of my own!) and spirituality. Finally, I was regaining my confidence. I was no longer blaming anyone for the situation. I was just trying to do my best.

When the results were declared, I really missed my grandpa. He would have been the happiest and proudest of us all. But somewhere deep down, I knew he had become my angel who did a special sifarish (recommendation) for me up there.

## 16

# How It Feels to Fail and Then Finally Succeed

In the last chapter of Part 1, let's discuss if all this hard work, sacrifice and perseverance are worth it. I know most of you want to have a glimpse of my life after the results. On 30 May, when the results were declared, a new chapter of my life began. From staying in one place for years to travelling all over the country for felicitations, it felt like a dream. The kind of love, affection and honour that people bestowed was unimaginable. And I am deeply grateful to the Almighty for that.

But practically speaking, all this is temporary. What is permanent is the feeling of relief, satisfaction and happiness that comes from within when your hard work pays off. The thought of being able to pursue a field you had always dreamt of fills you with self-confidence, joy and peace. Amid all this attention one receives, it becomes extremely important to stay grounded and be grateful to all those who stood by you in difficult times.

But we all know that with the UPSC exam, there is a greater chance of failing than succeeding. I've been there in my first attempt. How did I handle failure and what did I learn from it?

## What I felt after I failed my first Prelims

When I returned from the examination hall attempting only 56 questions, I felt empty and extremely tense. I knew there was no chance of making it to the list. The predicted cutoff was around 92, and I needed 49 correct answers out of 56 to sail through. It was wishful thinking as I had made a few guesses. I somehow gathered the courage to still appear for the CSAT, which is just a qualifying exam. But deep down, I had already prepared to go for a second attempt. When I finally returned home tired, disappointed and unmotivated, it felt like the end of the world. I had worked extremely hard for two years, made so many sacrifices and borne so many challenges. The result was a failure. I felt cheated for not getting my due rewards. I cursed everything – the exam pattern, those extra agriculture questions asked – but truly I was cursing only myself. I had lost.

I had made a mistake by panicking when I saw that I knew only 35 questions in the first paper. As I have said before, I was so stressed and full of self-doubt that I didn't realize that most students only know about 35 questions and intelligently guess the others. I didn't even mark all the answers I was 50 per cent sure of. I had committed a big strategic mistake, not because I hadn't worked hard but because I had lost my confidence in the exam hall.

Afterwards, I thought over my failure again and again. I was full of guilt. Why did I not make educated guesses? It was then I realized the basic principles of failure. Failures never occur because of one reason. There are multiple reasons that leave their mark. I made up my mind to analyse my past preparation strategies deeply to plug the loopholes.

I listened to strategy videos of numerous toppers available online and talked to some seniors to understand what had gone wrong. In the next part, I have discussed comprehensively the mistakes I made.

## Forgiving yourself

As I came to terms with my performance, I learnt another important lesson. It is extremely important to forgive yourself and take every failure as an experience. It may sound clichéd, but experiencing failures helps you become the best version of yourself. The only catch here is that you have to be open to take on the blame and accept that it is natural to falter and that one can always come back better.

After a lot of analysis of the strategies of toppers, I deduced the Rules of the Game I had ignored while preparing the first time. I didn't merely focus on getting over my failure in the Prelims but also focused on improving my strategy for the Mains and Interview stage too. I have written down these rules in Part 2 of the book.

Looking back, I feel that this honest analysis and reflection converted my failure into success. This, combined with my extra hard work, commitment and dedication to improve upon my mistakes, led me to success. If you are merely testing your luck every single time with minor tweaks in your preparation, you are on the wrong track. After a good 10-day break, I started preparing again, this time with even more enthusiasm and determination to make up for the failed attempt.

# Part 2

# Rules of the Game

This part discusses the 'rules' to crack the UPSC CSE and other competitive exams. I put them together after failing in my first attempt and found that they made a huge difference the second time around. In this part, I'll touch on various aspects of the preparation, such as making a timetable, utilizing the breaks well and preparing an exam-day strategy by taking examples from my journey.

# 1

# How I Planned for My First Prelims – And What I Got Wrong

Here is a broad outline of my first few years of preparation so that it's easy to decipher what went wrong during my first attempt.

**My plan since 2018**

1. The final year of my engineering degree: I read the basic NCERT books of all subjects, did the first reading of *Indian Polity* by M. Laxmikanth and of Spectrum's *A Brief History of Modern India*, and gave the sociology notes available in the market a reading.

   The last two months of the final year were largely spent enjoying the last rung of college life.

   From 9 May 2019, I started attending classes

conducted by a local teacher in Patiala to receive guidance on how to go about my preparations.

2. From May 2019 to July 2019: I covered modern history and economics in my daily classes and read and marked Spectrum alongside. I revised the daily notes extensively (which involved a lot of googling) and studied some topics in more depth, as per the demands of the exam. For example, if a particular government scheme was discussed in class, I made sure to google it further and to note down important details like the ministry associated with the scheme and the special provisions for women, if any, along the lines of the questions from the previous years.

   Till July, I would attend two and a half hours of class daily and dedicate around six to seven hours to self-study.

3. From July 2019 onwards: I started taking the optional subject (sociology) classes alongside the GS subjects.

   These classes went on till December. I supplemented my notes with books (Haralambos, Ritzer, B.K. Nagla and the available online material). It took me some time to understand the concepts of sociology. Many things were entirely new to me, and the one reading I had done last year had faded from my memory already.

   Along with that, I completed the other GS subjects in class like polity and current affairs (of environment and science and technology). I also picked ancient and medieval history on my own to get done with the basic subjects as quickly as possible.

From January 2020 onwards, there were no sociology classes, and the attention was solely on GS. I completed the portions of geography, art and culture, current affairs and other subjects by March when the threat of COVID-19 loomed large and the lockdown was imposed. I returned home and completely relied on self-study from then onwards.

I knew that I had not done enough revisions, had not solved any mocks, and even the current affairs portion was only half complete. As mentioned earlier, the lack of planning really hurt my chances. It clearly reflected in my preparation.

I panicked a little and started attempting the mocks at night while utilizing the daytime to study further. I later realized this was a mistake – I should have solved the mocks in the actual examination time.

Moreover, I did not seriously analyse the answers after attempting the mocks. I just glanced at the wrong questions, and that was it. Therefore, I could not learn from my mistakes.

Luckily the exam was postponed, and I thought that given the extra time, I would be able to make it. But I again made the same mistakes and did not devise a plan for those four months. I wasted a lot of time figuring out what to do and when. Every time I started revising my notes for a subject, I felt like I was missing out on the other topics and tried finishing it quickly so that I could cover the maximum amount of ground. I focused on the quantity of material and not the quality – another big mistake.

Yet another error was not revising the books thoroughly and relying only on my classroom notes, which were essential but not sufficient.

The last nail in the coffin was picking fresh current affairs notes in the month before the Prelims. I gave them priority over solving mocks and did not go through the questions from the previous years.

It would not be wrong to say I committed a bunch of mistakes. I did some things right too. I used those extra months to make some comprehensive notes on the topics of the Mains examination and revised my optional subject thoroughly. I also made handwritten notes from a crash course on current affairs (available for free on YouTube).

While I was not lacking in hard work, my methodology was not right. I missed a few crucial things and neglected a few game rules. It affected my self-confidence on the day of the exam and despite possessing a good knowledge of the questions asked in the exam, I did not make guesses and could attempt only 56 of them.

In a nutshell, this is all that went wrong in the first attempt:
- Not completing the syllabus on time and rushing through a few subjects in the last few days
- Lack of proper revision: I had read the basic books while preparing but had completely neglected to revise them in the last few months and relied solely on my classroom notes.
- Not solving enough mock papers (I solved around 25 only), and not solving them in the proper time frame, which was 9.30–11.30 a.m. for Prelims
- No proper analysis of mocks (discussed in an upcoming chapter in detail)
- Picking up new material a few days before the exam
- Not reading newspapers religiously and relying only on compilations of news analysis and notes
- Completely shifting my source of current affairs revision: Throughout the year, I read the daily news analysis on coaching academy websites by downloading the PDFs and combining them into a Word document. But when it was time to revise, I picked a monthly magazine. My advice is that one must always revise from the source one has read twice or thrice before.
- Not going through the UPSC question bank extensively and seriously
- Not relaxing my mind the day before the Prelims and being surrounded by books the entire day

- Failing to carefully watch the talks by toppers and therefore not knowing crucial aspects like the skill of attempting MCQs, elimination techniques, guesswork, etc.
- Not practising answer writing; so even if I had cleared the Prelims, getting through the Mains would have been difficult

I was bound to fail. I knew right after the exam that I had no chance as I had attempted only 56 questions. And the cutoff was usually around 95 (+-3). So I needed only seven to eight wrong questions to get out of the list.

Given that I did not possess any supernatural accuracy, being practical was the only way out. And in retrospect, I am glad I failed badly – by 26 marks. If we fail by a close margin, we can conveniently attribute it to luck and may not feel the need to work extra hard. Also, having clarity just a day after the exam, I didn't have to wait for the result to plan my next innings. So if I had to fail, it was indeed the best way to fail.

I have already discussed in Part 1 how I felt after my first attempt. In the next chapter, I discuss the changes I made and how my new plan looked.

# 2

# My Plan 2.0 Post Prelims

As already discussed in Part 1, I knew I was not going to clear the 2020 Prelims, so I did not wait for the results and started preparing for the next attempt – this time in mission mode.

**Changes I made to my strategy:**

1. Analysed my Prelims performance: I went to each question repeatedly and saw some videos of paper analysis, which helped me get clarity on the portions I had missed during my preparation. By carefully watching the post-exam analysis, I discovered that it was not just hard work but also the right skill that was essential to attempting the paper. The right skill involves:

- attempting enough questions (more than 85 at least if your accuracy is that of an average person) to safeguard against the wrong guesses
- going through the question twice so as not to miss keywords like 'not correct'
- not being afraid of encountering a new question and using the elimination strategy, which means cancelling the options that you know can never be correct and then arriving at the right answer from the remaining options
- applying common sense and not underestimating your daily observations (some questions need no prior knowledge and can be solved by applying your mind's daily observations)

2. Took a week to make a plan: after going through videos by toppers and reflecting upon my mistakes in the paper, I made a detailed plan. **One big thing that helped me succeed later was that I applied my learnings to all the stages without giving extra focus to the stage at which I had failed. You should always plan for success.** I started preparing for the Mains examination because I realized that there had been gaps my preparation; I knew that even if I made it through the Prelims next time, it would not prove to be a rewarding experience if I was unable to clear the Mains.

**So another rule of the game is: Focus on all three stages and give equal time to all. Don't take any stage lightly irrespective of whether you have cleared it once or not, especially the Prelims stage.**

I have seen many aspirants failing their next attempt of the Prelims after writing one or two Mains exams. It wastes an entire year and, of course, an attempt. In an exam like the CSE, you cannot afford to take any stage for granted. This exam demands consistent hard work and a lot of practice every single time.

## The new plan

Here is what it looked like:

*October 2020–January 2021*

From the third week of October 2020 (10–15 days after Prelims) to the first week of January (when the Mains 2020 was scheduled, which I was not eligible to write), I prepared extensively for the Mains. I prepared in a manner as if I had to appear in the upcoming 2020 Mains in January. I assumed for some time that I had cleared my Prelims and so I focused on the Mains extensively.

For the next Prelims, my basics were already prepared. So I just read the newspapers and followed the daily news analysis for current affairs. I did these two things religiously without skipping even a single day, and if you remember from the previous chapters, this was missing during my first attempt.

For the Mains preparation, my first target was my optional subject. Until then, I had prepared haphazardly from multiple sources. In those two months, I prepared concise sociology notes from all the books and notes I had read until then. I studied sociology for most of the day. This later helped me clear my Mains with good marks.

With that, I started making subject-wise notes for the Mains from newspapers, especially the editorials and the daily news analysis available online. I took the printout and marked the portions relevant for the Prelims – remember the 'no excuses policy' chapter.

One additional thing I did was practise answer writing. I joined GS Mains test series 2020 and sociology test series 2020 since I had decided to prepare as if I was writing the Mains 2020. In November, I attempted four answers from those GS test papers daily.

I did not start attempting the full mocks because I knew it was more important to enrich the quality of the answers. I dedicated an hour exclusively to writing the answers and self-evaluating them. When I completed 20 answers, I would send the test for evaluation. This continued until the first week of December. I was almost done with sociology note-making and revision when I started attempting the three-hour part tests of sociology (in which a portion of the syllabus was tested).

Along with that, I made notes of the GS Mains topics that were in addition to the Prelims, e.g., GS 3 and GS 4. I kept four different sections in a notebook for each GS paper and a separate notebook for the optional and essays. I kept noting the relevant points from newspapers as per the syllabus. This way, the revisions before my Mains examination became very easy and systematic.

**I made sure to prepare concise notes in a bullet-point format, similar to the structure of an answer.**

By the first week of January, I had revised self-made sociology notes, had written three-part test papers of the subject (that covered 70 per cent of the syllabus) and practised three to four questions daily from the GS 1–4 papers.

It took me four hours initially to complete a sociology test, and over time, I got better. So, no need to panic if you cannot complete the paper on time in the initial days. I also kept referring to the answer sheets of toppers from the previous years to get an idea of what constitutes a good answer. Meanwhile, in these two months, I also kept solving 10 MCQs daily (available online – both current and static) to be in touch with the Prelims, and this practice continued until I appeared in the Prelims exam.

## *January–March 2021*

After the Mains 2020 was conducted, I analysed the questions and solved them. I felt more comfortable after these three months of work. Let's look at the changes from mid-January onwards:

- I shifted to revising the static portions for both the Prelims and the Mains. I finalized my book list and stuck to those books for preparing static. I have discussed the book list at the end. This time, besides reading the books, I made sure to memorize them thoroughly.
- Since January, I had taken two Prelims test series, one of which was a crash course cum test, to ensure that I didn't miss any important topic. I completed all the basic sources by mid-March and was on schedule with the test series.
- I continued with the analysis of the newspapers and daily news in the background, while also preparing notes from the newspapers for the Mains.

## *March–May 2021*

By mid-March, I was done with the first revision of the book list. The UPSC had scheduled the Prelims for the end of May. I had two and a half months and I dedicated most of my time preparing for it.

- I started with the revision of current affairs (relying on my daily news analysis printouts and extra newspaper notes of items I had missed in the news analysis). With that, the second revision of the book list was complete.
- I had started solving the weekly tests of two test series. By April end, I had completed 70 per cent of my current affairs and was done with my second revision. It was time to shift to the question papers of the previous years and solve a mock paper from 9.30 to 11.30 a.m. every day.

But as the COVID-19 cases started increasing, there was an indication of the paper getting postponed. That derailed my preparation a bit and I got delayed in starting my full-day mocks. By mid-May, the news was confirmed. The exams had been shifted by four months.

At first, it came as a relief, but then I found it very hard to sustain my momentum. I often felt demotivated and impatient. I had been putting in 9–10 hours daily since my first Prelims and was impatient for the exam to be over. But here I was, with no end in sight and having to study current affairs for an additional four months.

I took a few days off when I heard the exams had been postponed. But I was constantly restless. I was scared to slip into my comfort zone. This fear was eating away at my productivity, and I could neither enjoy my free time nor study. When you have failed once, the sheer thought of losing again due to your own inefficiency keeps you anxious.

My parents advised me not to be too harsh on myself and take proper breaks, but I didn't listen to them. The calmness, the positivity and the patience I had exhibited until now began to crumble. It took me a few days of introspection, crying and irritation to finally follow my parents' advice.

I reduced my study hours to seven hours a day and extended my break timings to ease the pressure I was feeling.

## *June 2021*

From June, I shifted my focus to the Mains again as I wanted to use this extra time to improve my answers. I joined an essay-ethics test series and a sociology test series. This also helped me to refresh my mind, which was tired of reading the same material again and again.

I started writing weekly complete tests of sociology, essays and ethics papers. I gave three sociology tests after revision, three essay tests (which is six essays as each test consists of two essays) and three ethics papers of three hours each. I also took proper breaks in between and went to meet my friends for a couple of days (for the first time since October 2019). Meeting them instilled new energy and confidence in me.

## *July–September 2021*

From July end onwards, I started revising the static and the current portions, and from the beginning of August, I began solving the daily mock tests of different institutes available online.

I solved one paper on alternate days and analysed it thoroughly. I ensured that I incorporated the learnings in my next revision and read carefully the points I had missed.

From September, I started giving one paper each day and went to a nearby school to get accustomed to the surroundings of an examination hall. I have discussed in the next chapter how the environment where we attempt the mock paper becomes extremely relevant. I continued revising the syllabus side by side and added the test solutions to the revision list.

## *October – just before the exam*

By early October, I stopped attempting daily mock papers. During the 10 days before the exam, I did not pick any new material and instead focused on extensive revisions and went through the questions from the previous years. For static subjects like history, polity and geography, **I solved the question bank since the 1990s, going away from the common perception that only the questions asked post-2013 should be kept in mind.** This extensive solving of previous years questions (PYQs) helped me to get into the right mindset for solving UPSC-style MCQs.

## How do PYQs help?

We must analyse every question and study every option given for a particular question. Sometimes in the exam a new question could pop up from these options. Do not try to memorize the answers. Instead, analyse the answer keys thoroughly to understand what kind of answers are considered correct by the UPSC. Most often, candidates have doubts about two options and are stuck there, not knowing which answer will be acceptable to the UPSC. I received help from PYQs to solve this dilemma as I had thoroughly studied which answer was considered correct as per the UPSC answer key. It helped me make more calculated guesses when handling confusing options. So studying and analysing PYQs will help you predict the demand of the examination and identify important topics that are the favourites of the UPSC.

PYQs should not be set aside for the last stage of preparation. Instead, at every juncture, they can help you from going off-track. Before and after every revision, you must refer to the PYQs to not divert your attention away from important topics. In my second attempt, I solved the PYQs extensively. The PYQs remain equally important even at the Mains and Interview stage and help you in terms of what is necessary and what is not, what to read and what to skip.

Hence, the crucial takeaways would be:
1. Solving UPSC PYQs question bank extensively
2. Not reading anything new in the last few days before the exam

# 3

# How Many Hours of Study Do You Need?: A Sneak Peek into My Timetable

Though there is no strict number, given how extensive and bulky the syllabus is, I believe eight to nine hours of serious study every day is a must. In case you are a super genius or from some other planet, three or four hours might be good for you. But being a normal human being, I had to sometimes extend to 11–12 hours of study a day.

One lesson I learnt from my first attempt was that we must not include the coaching class time in the study time and fool ourselves. **Putting in good hours of self-study is vital.** If you put in fewer hours, you may end up compromising either the quantity or the quality of work.

Of course, you can't just keep staring at the clock and wait for the eight hours to be over. The purpose is to do some effective study that really counts. I am a morning person, so my productivity was maximum in that slot of time. I used to get up at 4.45 a.m., irrespective of any circumstance. You do not need to forcefully get up early if you think that your mind is most active during the night hours.

Chalk out your own timings. I avoided taking long breaks in the first half of the day. A 10-minute break after an hour worked for me. My mind would be fresh and I knew that if I got up for a long break, it would be difficult to go back to my studies with the same energy. With that, I would finish three and a half hours of study by 9.30 a.m. The distractions in this slot were zero. I avoided interacting even with family members and kept the phone far away from my sight. I even steered clear of googling in this slot; instead, I would note down the points I had to research for later.

Then I would take a half-hour break, in which I would have what I called my mini breakfast of fruits and some vegetables. Having successfully sailed through the first slot of the day, I would feel relieved and satisfied.

From here onwards, I decreased the study slots and increased the break slots. From 10 a.m. to 12 p.m., I studied for an hour and a half hours with two 15-minute breaks.

And then came my main mealtime, which included a long break from 12 to 1 p.m., as I had already studied for a good five hours.

The slot after the break was from 1 to 3.30 p.m. during which I would manage to study for an hour and a half hours. My efficiency during the period would be low, so I would take some breaks in between. It's fine to study properly for 20 minutes and rejuvenate with a 5–10 minutes break. Basically, you must analyse how your mind works, when it can do without breaks and when it is inevitable you take a good long break.

By 3.30 p.m., I would have studied for six and a half hours. And then came the best part of the day. A long refreshing slot of an hour and a half to two hours – this is when I would have a short nap and a good time over a cup of tea with my parents, who would be back from the office by then.

Before 3.30 p.m., I would be mostly by myself with almost no interaction with anyone. Sometimes I would chat with my brother, who worked from home, but I avoided gossiping.

At 5.30 p.m., it would be time for another slot, and it was the most difficult one for me. I struggled to leave the chitchat and return to my room on the first floor. The technique I used was an annoying alarm ringtone on my phone, which I deliberately left on the stairs that took me to my room. Once I got up to shut the blasting alarm, my inertia would dissipate and I would gather the strength to return to my studies.

From 5.30 to 7.30 p.m., I either revised a portion or glanced at the answer sheets of the toppers from the previous years. It is not a good idea to pick a new topic when your concentration is low. I studied for an hour and a half hours in that slot.

So by 7.30 p.m., I had spent eight hours studying seriously. The Smarter Time app would be my constant companion throughout the day, making me cautious of the time I was wasting unknowingly.

My favourite slot was 7.30 to 8.30 p.m., when I spent my time walking, eating dinner and listening to light music. It was the only time I met some people from the colony, who were also out for their walk.

My last slot of 8.30 to 10 p.m. I dedicated to reading the daily news analysis and solving 10 daily MCQs for the Prelims.

This was what my average day looked like.

On the days I felt the need to push harder, I would steal time from the afternoon break of two hours (remember: 3.30–5.30 p.m.!) and cut short the walk time on some days to compensate.

I sincerely suggest you not copy this timetable entirely or do so at your own risk. If you copy it, you might be doing a great injustice to yourself. Make a schedule that suits *you*. One thing you must borrow from my experience is following your timetable religiously. I made sure to stick to it every day. Yes, you read it right – every day!

You might study for two hours at a stretch and relax for half an hour or study for half an hour with a five-minute break – it doesn't matter at all. Stop wasting your energy on making that perfect timetable and start studying. The schedule will follow as you realize what ensures your maximum productivity.

Framing a timetable is only one half of the issue; the other more difficult half is sticking to it. The question that troubles us is, 'What should we do when we don't meet our daily targets?'

There is no sure-shot answer to this complicated question. But I will try to share the techniques that worked for me.

So, when I decided to wake up at 5 a.m., an hour and a half hours earlier than my schedule of 6.30 a.m., I believed it would just take me an alarm to achieve it. I had completely neglected the hidden devil – my laziness.

However determined you may be when you go to bed, when the alarm rings in the morning, getting up feels like the most difficult task in the world. When I suddenly changed my alarm time, I realized I could not get up. Instead, I started missing my 6.30 a.m. alarm too.

One common thought that makes it even more difficult is, *'15–20 mins main kaun sa pahaad chadh lenge'* (No big deal in losing 15–20 minutes). I had miserably failed to achieve my own established target. What did I do about it?

I followed an approach that slowly developed this habit. I dropped the idea of getting up 5 a.m. and instead started with a 6.15 a.m. alarm, 15 minutes earlier than my usual time. It was a lot easier, and I gave myself about three to four days to settle into this time. Soon, I shifted the alarm to 6 a.m. and repeated the same cycle.

It gave me a psychological boost of having done something better each day and, eventually, in a month and a half, I could reach the desired 5 a.m. target. So, the lesson I learnt was that if we rush with things, they are most likely to remain temporary. It is a myth that we should and can develop good habits in haste. Giving some time is necessary and worth it.

The same principle applies to other daily targets too. When I consecutively missed my target some days, I felt guilty and helpless. **It was because I had set the bar too high, targeting the maximum possible rather than the comfortably doable. I observed that it was impacting my mindset negatively. So I started lowering the targets and realized what I could achieve comfortably by giving my best.**

It might sound counterproductive to surrender to the mind, but believe me, it does more good than harm. When you start achieving your targets, it pushes you to put in extra effort and raise the bar. It becomes an interesting game for you.

I did not have nine hours of study as my initial target. I started with six to six and a half hours, and soon progressed to seven, seven and a half and then eight. I stopped at eight hours and anything above that was a bonus. You stay happier and more positive by achieving that half- or one-hour bonus, than keeping your target of nine hours and missing it by 15 minutes.

Also, try keeping a record of each day, irrespective of whether or not you have achieved that daily target. I used to mark a tick along with the number of hours on my calendar. This practice will make it easier for you to see if there is more scope to push yourself, and you can be happy about all the days you could achieve your target.

# 4

# How to Plan Your Breaks

It is very important to use your break slots effectively. The purpose is not to entertain yourself but to be rejuvenated and ready for the next study slot. So do not waste your break slots by engaging in random chitchat, only to realize later that the mind and the body are still tired. There is no single ideal way to take a good break – you need to figure out what helps you regain the lost energy.

But some things are better avoided. For the short break slots of 15–20 minutes:
1. Do not dial a friend. Most likely, it will take longer than expected, making you feel guilty later.
2. Avoid getting into time-consuming discussions with family members. You should tell them clearly that you are not interested in listening about anything happening around you.

I would get very irritated when told about some incident involving a random neighbour, which consumed five minutes of my precious break time. You cannot expect them to know when you are interested in a conversation and when you are not, so just tell them.
3. Do not scroll on Instagram or Facebook. It takes about three minutes, but its after-effects on the mind linger. You might feel 'FOMO' when you see really fun parties or trips or go into that comparison mode every time your friends share their new achievements. It's better to avoid anything that causes mental trouble.

I relied heavily on music and would pair it with some exercise. Or I would go to the balcony for some fresh air. Sometimes, I watched a short YouTube clip or the trailers of upcoming movies.

## For the one-hour break slot

You may combine your meal time with watching TV or anything on your laptop. Avoid starting a new movie or web series. However determined you may be, the chances of returning to your books in the middle of a gripping plot are thin. After all, dil to bachcha hai ji! (Our heart still longs for something, like that of a kid!) I relied on the movies I had already seen, so that it didn't bother me if I had to leave it in between. And if your family is around, choose to have at least one meal together at the dinner table. It helps in calming the mind.

Another way could be to go to an area close to nature for a walk.

## In the two-hour break slot

I would nap for 20–25 minutes, chitchat with the family and share the accumulated frustrations of the day with them. It worked as my booster for the day. Sometimes I would call a friend in this time slot.

Whenever I decided to take a half-day (once in 14–15 days) or a full-day break (once a month), I would go to some nearby cafe or visit the local shops for a change of environment. I avoided any activity that could linger on for the next day, like staying up late at night (that would mean getting up late the next day, creating a disturbance in the entire schedule) or travelling out of town, which could tire me.

Instead of going out for dinner, go out for lunch so that you don't compromise on your sleep time. And instead of watching a new movie in the theatre, just use your laptop to do so. It saves you travel time. Also stealing time from here and there becomes extremely essential in this journey. These small changes count, and when allowed to multiply they produce a beautiful result.

So, the takeaway here is that each and every minute becomes crucial. Breaks should neither be avoided nor wasted. Instead, they should be planned in such a way that they lead to the productive use of time. Do not feel guilty about taking offs when needed – you need to be smart enough to choose an activity that is the least distracting. Breaks are essential, and rewarding yourself frequently for your efforts is extremely important.

Remember: If there was no diastole (the rest phase between two heartbeats), the heart that beats all our lives would give up in a single day!

# 5

# How Important Is It to Solve Mocks?

One crucial reason for my failure was not attempting enough mocks. The ones I solved were not attempted seriously within a time frame. I had not spent time going over my performance after every mock and was lost in my assumption that these marks in the mocks were in no way a replica of the official exam marks.

During my second attempt, I was very careful not to make a mockery of the mocks!

I joined two Prelims test series in January 2021 to maintain discipline and plan my revision as per the official test. One was a normal test series, and the other was a crash-course-cum-test series with some introductory video lectures before the mock.

I followed both test series religiously. The video lectures

helped me remember the topics I had missed during the preparation. I studied them extensively and prepared my notes for them, especially the dynamic subjects like science, technology and economics.

The tests were weekly, so I got enough time to prepare well. **It's important to attempt a mock after a good revision, as it gives you a clear picture of where you stand.**

I had planned to attempt daily mocks from 9.30 to 11.30 a.m. mid-April onwards. But when the exam was rescheduled, I shifted this plan to the start of August. In August, I attempted one mock paper every day from different academies.

## How to give your mocks

For the Prelims (or any other competitive exam), you need to train your mind to give its best at 9.30 a.m. sharp (or the official exam time). You can achieve it by solving one paper daily at the allotted time.

**Even when you are not giving a mock at 9.30 a.m., avoid distractions until 11.30 a.m., and be mentally very alert for at least a month before the exam.** Don't talk to anyone or take a nap during that two hours' time, so that your mind gets accustomed to giving its best in that duration.

The conditions in which you attempt the mock also become extremely important. I would advise you to avoid the room you study in. Its familiarity doesn't prepare you well for the unfamiliar atmosphere of the examination hall. Rather, go to a not very comfortable table and chair so that these things don't matter in the exam hall.

I would go to a nearby government school every weekend two months before the exam and attempt the paper sitting on a bench far from the fan and light. I would ask my brother or father to come in and disturb me a bit because the exam hall is not always as silent as you would want it to be. I would tell them to get an attendance sheet and get my signatures so that the time it takes is also taken into account.

These small changes help you feel a little more relaxed and calmer in the actual exam, especially for first-timers with no first-hand experience.

I always made sure to take a good break after the mock exam before I started analysing it. You should always analyse with a fresh mind. A tired body and a tired mind can never draw good insights, thus defeating the purpose of the exercise! I would get a proper neck massage before the next innings.

And one more important message here is to never take the marks to heart, especially in the initial mocks. I started with a score of 85 and towards the end could score 110–115 on average. Just try to get a few more marks the next time, and if you are unable to improve, give serious thought to what could be the mistakes. Maybe it's the lack of revision, or negative marking due to random guesses, or time management. You must figure out the reason through constant evaluation. Even if you score badly in the last mocks, do not get disheartened. The actual exam questions will be different. Besides, you will only be making yourself nervous by lowering your self-confidence.

I got test papers from multiple institutes as it is good to have a diversity of questions.

## Mocks become equally important for the UPSC Mains

My exam was scheduled to be held in the winter, and it became an additional hurdle. I made sure to switch off the heaters while giving the final mock tests. I practised in the same school and purposely chose the coldest room with the least sunlight. It helped me step out of my comfort zone and experience a cold and disagreeable environment. I planned my attire accordingly.

**I also tried three different jackets during three separate mocks and then chose the most comfortable one out of them.** I believe it gave me an edge in the actual exam as I heard aspirants discussing their inability to write in their ill-suited, heavyweight jackets.

I had missed a few questions during preparation and the mocks helped me cover those as well.

In this manner, mocks not only help us evaluate our current standing but also train our minds beforehand to give our best in the actual exam. We become better prepared for surprises and feel more confident about dealing with unexpected situations.

## How many mocks must you attempt?

I attempted some 70–75 full and sectional mock tests during the Prelims stage, and for the Mains, I wrote about four or five 3-hour papers for each GS exam. That adds up to 20 tests for GS 1, 2, 3 and 4. Additionally, I wrote six essay tests (which is 12 essays as one test has two essay topics) and an additional four ethics tests. For the optional exam, sociology, I wrote twelve 3-hour tests. It was in addition to some daily answers I wrote for practice.

Attempting a lot of mock papers for the Prelims becomes important due to these reasons:
1. When the brain goes through the same state repeatedly; it sharpens its axe. By solving many MCQs, it opens the memory box and retrieves the disc related to MCQ tricks. The next time you see a question, you will take a few seconds less to get accustomed to it, and your mind will automatically start searching for the right answers.

2. It improves guesswork and increases the confidence to solve the question despite not knowing the right answer beforehand. Your mind gets trained to push further and explore even when it is unsure of the answer.
3. When you solve the paper in the same timeframe, with proper Optical Mark Recognition (OMR) filling, it saves you from panicking in the examination hall. Your mind already knows how to adjust to the remaining time. You are well prepared and know the time it will take to fill the OMR Sheet. It will save you from an adrenaline rush and help in using the last few minutes well as you have already been trained to handle the pressure.
4. Mocks prepare you for every scenario, like staying calm when the first few questions seem out of the box. There will be tests where you do not know the first 15 questions and yet score above 120. And others where you know the first 20 questions so well that it makes you overconfident and you end up with a lot of negative marking. Or where you over-attempt and unnecessarily make a lot of guesses, ending up with your name getting dropped off the list.

The other scenario that I faced was when I knew a good number of questions, and in that excitement I made very silly mistakes.

So, mocks train you well for different scenarios, ensuring you will be less surprised in the examination hall.

It is always better to commit as many mistakes beforehand and learn not to repeat them in the examination hall. Mocks have the potential to polish the surface repeatedly to reveal the real gem beneath, which both the UPSC and you are seeking!

For this mental training to be complete, I would evaluate my performance in the mocks. I would make three columns:

1. The number of sure-shot questions (whose answers I felt I absolutely knew) I ticked and how many I got correct
2. Questions I had guessed with two options known
3. Questions I had guessed with one option known
4. Questions where I had made wild guesses

To my amazement, I would always score a good 5–6 marks with wild guesses by merely paying attention to the wording of the statement.

That pushed me to not leave the questions that were completely unknown to me. Sometimes just reading the statement gives an intuition if we use our holistic knowledge, and that intuition becomes stronger with practice.

Another pattern I found was that I always got about

four to five sure-shot answers incorrect in the section I felt I absolutely knew the answers to, which reduced my ultimate score. This happened either because I made mistakes while marking the OMR or did not read the question carefully. I improved on it by ensuring that I read the question twice and very carefully underlined the 'keywords' so that I did not get the gist of the question wrong.

This exercise helped me decide the optimum number of questions that I must attempt, ranging from 90 to 95, and maximize my score. I believe it's risky to attempt less than 85 questions, as you leave a lot to chance that way.

Make sure you do the post-mock analysis within two days of taking the exam. After that, one's memory fades, and you are most likely to forget what pushed you to mark a particular option in the first place. Then the whole exercise becomes futile.

In the post-exam analysis, go to every question you got wrong, study the thought process that made you mark that option and ensure you register the mistake in your mind well enough not to repeat it. Mind your MIND!

Then go to every correct answer and see what worked; sometimes it's not what you thought but just luck that got you the marks. So, correct your thought process there. Then finally go to the questions you skipped and memorize their answers. After this exercise, you will bridge the gap in the content and be able to learn any topic that you may have missed. It helps you to analyse the topics that you are still unprepared for or are out of your memory and need more attention. You can get to know your strengths and weaknesses and improve upon them. It also helps to revise better, as you get a fair idea of the topics that need more attention.

In my case, I got two questions straight from the test series. Thanks to proper analysis and the habit of memorizing anything new that came up, I got the correct answers, and it made a huge difference. I would get a printout of the solved answers to highlight the extra content and revise it before the actual exam.

**Many times, questions from previous exams might not get repeated but new questions can be framed from those answers. So, reading and memorizing the detailed answers becomes crucial, even for the questions you got right.**

Assuming that you have thoroughly read the questions from the previous years, you will know what to mark and register in the brain after a glance at the analysis.

For the Mains too, writing mocks is crucial as:
1. In the Mains, it becomes tricky to put your vast knowledge across in a few words. You might have enough depth and hold over topics, but when it comes to meeting the exact demand of the question, one

tends to divert from the topic or exceed the word limit. Hence, for your mind to think, brainstorm and write simultaneously within the time, you need to train it, which the mocks help in doing.

2. You can practise different ways of writing – point form, paragraph style, flow charts, diagrams – and try multiple structures beforehand and analyse what can fetch the maximum marks. I initially started writing in paragraph form and realized that it consumed a lot of time and space and made it difficult to touch upon multiple dimensions. So, I finally shifted to point format (writing the arguments point-wise). You must decide what suits you best. And practice papers help you make this decision.

3. The quality of answers improves when you write multiple tests and analyse them well. Every time you write a test, go back to it and think about what else you could have incorporated into your answer. And when you revise your notes, keep the questions you attempted in mind and look for relevant examples or case studies to quote. In this way, slowly, you can enrich your content.

4. Test papers help you get accustomed to sitting continuously for three hours. Such tests prepare the body for the battle in the exam hall. One must attempt the three-hour papers and should not just rely on the practice of writing a few questions daily. It's

about getting accustomed to writing continuously for three hours and deriving equal productivity from that last one hour when your hand is aching and your energy levels start dropping. Each question is equally important and must not be compromised.

5. It helps one to manage time appropriately. In the Mains, completing the paper on time is extremely important, and given how long the paper is, only through repeated practice can one develop this habit. Sometimes, we become so engrossed in making our answers better, we forget to keep an eye on the clock. In CSE, this mistake can cost you an attempt. You must attempt all the questions, as that extra effort to beautify your 19 answers cannot compensate for the 3–4 marks you could get on an average after attempting the twentieth question.

To sail through the Interview stage, mock interviews again become very important.

Until this stage, we don't rehearse speaking our viewpoints. Mock interviews break that inertia and prepare you for probable questions you might face on the actual day. They help you rehearse wearing formal attire, which could be a new experience for some.

To sum up, consistently solving multiple mock papers is that rule of the game, which, if ignored, is sure to invite failure.

# 6

# How to Read Newspapers Effectively

You can't do without newspapers in an exam like the CSE. I made the mistake of ignoring and bypassing them in my first attempt, which was a failure. No news analysis can compensate for the newspapers. Newspapers can be read in multiple ways, and in the CSE too, you must read your newspaper in different ways for the three stages.

**For the Prelims**

The key areas to focus on are facts, data points, terms (especially for economics) and the static background behind the current news. You need to explore these points in detail. Say you read an article that mentions a particular tribal movement from the period of the freedom struggle.

Newspapers might not elaborate on it, but it becomes your duty to explore it further and prepare all the relevant questions that could be framed out of that topic for the Prelims. If it's covered in the daily news analysis you follow, well and good. Otherwise, make sure to google it further, and make a small note. In a newspaper what is relevant and what is not is a question that troubles many candidates. The only way out of this dilemma is to look at the questions from the previous years, which give you an idea about the frequently asked topics and how in-depth your preparation should be.

Also, for the Prelims, anything that you study in the static book must be correlated with the current news.

## For the Mains

The focus must be on analysing a particular topic from different angles. If there is a topic that can be debated upon, you must understand both sides of the issue thoroughly and form a balanced opinion. The editorial pages are extremely helpful for the Mains. You must analyse every article correlating with the topics in your Mains syllabus and mentally structure answers for questions likely to be asked from the topic.

Whenever I made my notes on different topics from newspapers, I wrote them in an answer format, inserting the data quoted in the newspaper article in the introduction, other points in the body and the suggestions in the conclusion.

This way, I made my work easy for the Mains. A diversity of points becomes very important for this exam. You should not just stick to one angle and keep explaining it, but explain the same topic from different angles – political, social, environmental, ethical, economic, etc.

The conclusions must always be optimistic and forward-looking and show there is good scope for improvement in a given situation.

## For the Interview

Newspapers become 80 per cent of your preparation at this stage. For the Prelims and the Mains, I followed only one newspaper. But for the Interview stage, I started reading three newspapers: *The Hindu*, *The Indian Express* and *The Tribune* (for the regional news).

For the Interview, every news in and around your area becomes important. The focus should not be on memorizing the facts but on framing your own opinions on every issue. I started watching a few discussions daily on different news channels, like Sansad TV, to understand different opinions, and based on the knowledge I had gained during the preparation, I framed my opinion.

Remember, your opinion and viewpoint must be logical, optimistic and balanced. You can take the backing of the Constitution and the Supreme Court judgements on some controversial issues. At this stage, the newspapers must be followed until the last day, even the news of the day of the Interview becomes crucial.

Though we have newspapers inside the UPSC hall where we are seated before going into the Interview room, I did not want to leave them for the last. What if my Interview was immediately after I entered the hall? So, I arranged for newspapers locally before going to the venue and just read the headlines. You need not go very deep, as you would already know the context if you have been following the news. Just take account of any new developments and make sure you read the headlines of regional news too.

I developed the habit of newspaper reading in my college days. I would recommend all beginners start with this aspect of preparation first. Make the newspaper your best friend. Initially, it would take me nearly two and a half hours to finish reading the day's papers, so do not worry if you take more time in the early days. Slowly, the time I took reduced to 45 minutes. I got immense help from my father in covering the newspaper portions. I read the newspaper a day late, as my father would mark the essential points every day and the next day, I would read it and focus on the marked items.

I ignored the points I felt were not very relevant. But since my father had also read all my GS books, he had a good idea of what was important.

# 7

# What to Do One Day before the Prelims

Here's a list of things to pursue one day before:
1. Do deep breathing and close your eyes. (I'm not a person who likes to meditate, so this was my way to calm myself.)
2. Stay quiet and preserve your energy. Do not take it as a free day, where you are not studying and can talk about random things and gossip. I used to speak very little on the day before the exams. It helped me conserve energy and sharpen my focus.
3. Smile a lot. Yes, it makes a difference by generating refreshing vibes and by taking you away from tensions and worries.
4. Visit a park or a spiritual place to soothe your mind and give it the space it needs to work at full speed the

next day. I had my exams in Chandigarh and there was a park near the place I stayed.

5. Eat a very light diet, especially dinner. A heavy dinner makes one feel lethargic. So, I avoided taking anything fried or spicy and relied mainly on dal and chapati, with no sweet dish.

6. Count the reasons that make you deserve success. Revisit the days you studied hard and the challenges you overcame in the journey, and send a positive message to yourself – that you deserve it and will get it.

    I made it a point to tell myself again and again that 'I deserve it'. Never criticize yourself or feel guilty about leaving some topics. At this stage, you must trust your preparation and pay attention to what you have done.

7. Visit the examination centre to get accustomed so that the time taken to adapt to the surroundings decreases the next day.

8. In the first half, instead of revising some random notes, take a look at the questions from the PYQs again, specifically the ones asked in the last six years. In my case, I googled the environment question bank of 2010–13 and thoroughly read all the options in the answer. I got one question from that googled option and managed to secure 2 additional marks.

9. Go to bed early so that you get eight to nine hours of solid sleep.

One way to soothe your nerves is to tell yourself that whatever you have not studied will not come. But I knew that wasn't true as in the UPSC you cannot expect to have read about more than 50 questions.

So, the message I gave myself was that no matter what, I will be able to solve the questions from the topics I hadn't read if I stay calm and apply my knowledge carefully. Most of the time, the questions require just a simple application of the facts or basic concepts, and sometimes the answers are hidden inside the questions. That requires calm focus and self-belief. So, it didn't scare me when something entirely new came up in the exam.

## Things NOT to do one day before the Prelims

1. Learning new facts/data or picking any new material
2. Solving a mock paper: The marks in the mock paper can affect the actual performance and even shake your confidence.
3. Checking your mobile phone: There's no need to reply to 'All The Best' messages on WhatsApp, Instagram, SMS or Telegram. I made it a point to stop checking any messages or calls a day before the exam so that nothing diverted my attention. You cannot allow any distractions to get in the way.
4. Eating spicy or junk food
5. Sleeping late or getting up too early

6. Travelling on the day of the exam: Try as much as possible to arrive a day before to the city where your centre is located.
7. Revising in the second half of the day: Your mind needs to be clear before the exam, and if you keep it occupied the entire day with loads of stuff to memorize, you might not be able to decipher the hidden answers in the exam.

## The D-day – Prelims

On the day of the exam, we expect everything to be super smooth. But things don't always work as per our plans.

For me, the day was anything but normal. I had slept at 10.30 p.m. the previous night with the alarm set for 6.30 a.m., planning a good eight hours of sleep. But at 3.30 a.m., I woke up with severe pain in the neck; I couldn't even turn it. It had become stiff because of the pillow in the new room – and my cervical problem had made it worse.

Did I panic? Yes. My sleep was incomplete. I wasn't able to look down due to my rigid muscles, and on top of it, the pain had begun to move to my right arm. It felt like I was going to lose.

But I gathered all my courage and decided to rise to the challenge and not panic. I woke up my parents, and we tried to do what was best possible – got some hot water bottles, a muscle relaxant medicine and a soft massage to reduce the stiffness. The takeaway here is not to let panic take a toll on the senses but figure out the best possible alternative.

It took me some time to process the entire incident, but thanks to the Almighty I stayed strong enough and even managed to laugh at the turn of events. That is something I suggest to all of you. Laugh at the sudden hitches and do not let them take control of you. Had I given up in that moment, I would have lost the game even before attempting the exam.

I knew that nothing except my attitude was in my control. After an hour of discomfort, I managed to get two hours of sleep and woke up at 7 a.m. The neck was still stiff but better.

I told everyone around not to ask me about the neck and arm pain because it would unnecessarily remind me that there was something wrong. I had a light breakfast of sweet daliya and sandwiches. I filled my water bottles – one with room-temperature water and the other with glucose water. A sip of glucose whenever I felt mentally tired helped me regain my concentration.

I didn't keep chocolate with me because opening the packet and chewing it, and in the process, perhaps staining my hand if it melted would consume some precious time, which I could not afford. Every second inside the exam hall is important. I didn't want to take any risk whatsoever.

On the day of the exam, there are a few minor yet important things to be kept in mind:

1. Reach the exam centre at least half an hour before to get accustomed to the environment, and keep enough of a margin to check your bench and ask for a replacement if needed. I know of some aspirants who arrived late by a few minutes, and that cost them a full year as they were denied entry.

2. Do not talk to any other aspirant, specifically about any syllabus-related things or about the number of questions to be attempted. Just stay quiet and breathe deeply.

3. Never mess with the invigilators. Just present your demands very politely, and if they refuse, do not get into any arguments. At that moment, your mental peace is extremely important and you can't let anyone spoil it.

   Sometimes the invigilators might question you about 'which attempt is it' and you might react without realizing the impact it can have. It's best to ignore such questions. Don't unnecessarily spoil your mood because of anything unimportant happening in your exam centre.

4. Carry a watch and an extra black pen. During my

attempt, I saw a few aspirants looking for the right pen to mark the attendance sheet or asking the invigilators about the time left, which I feel is avoidable through proper planning.

5. Keep all your prejudices away. In my first attempt (which was unsuccessful) my sheet code was C, and in the second attempt, it was again C, and for a moment I did think of that as unlucky. But I clearly remember how I changed my way of thinking and reasserted that everything might be the same as the last time, but the result need not be so!

   So, there is no lucky/unlucky room, position, centre or sheet code. These things are just in your head.

6. Finally, when you start answering the question paper, make sure that you don't panic seeing the first 10 questions, even if you don't know a single one.

   I had prepared myself for the situation and assumed that I might not know 'N' number of questions in the very first go. So, when there were a few questions from the sports section in the initial pages that I didn't know, I could still control my mind. One thing I had taught myself repeatedly was that the exam is subjective – I don't need to get above a fixed threshold; I just need to do slightly better than the others to get myself on the list.

   I knew I had prepared honestly and maintained

full faith that if I felt the paper was tough, it would be the same for 90 per cent of the aspirants. In other words, I'm in the same boat as the others and am safe that way.

This was a major deviation I made from my first attempt. During the first attempt, I had lost my confidence upon encountering some unexpected questions. I started questioning my preparation within the exam hall and forgot that it was the same for all, so I did not attempt even the questions I could have by taking calculated risks.

7. Avoid going back to the questions you have marked already, even if it is guesswork. Generally, the first guess that the mind makes is the best. And if you revisit every guessed question, you will not be able to go through the entire paper.

8. Mark the OMR sheet carefully, without panicking. It is better not to leave it for last. What I did was, after the first reading of the paper, which took me around 50 minutes, I marked on the OMR sheet the answers I had ticked on the question paper. These were 35–40 questions. After that, I marked the options side by side to avoid making any mistakes.

When we keep the exercise of 'marking bubbles' to the end, it creates pressure on the mind, and we are most likely to make mistakes and lose precious marks.

9. Use the last 15 minutes very cautiously. Quickly estimate the number of questions you have attempted and make only calculated guesses. Don't lose control over your nerves and over-attempt. At the same time, do not be too afraid to mark. You must maintain the same calmness you had in the first 15 minutes. As already discussed, if you have practised well with the mock papers, this won't be a problem for you.

After submitting the OMR sheet, do not go over the paper. Just relax, eat something and concentrate on the CSAT. You cannot take it lightly. So ensure that you are not overconfident. There is also no need to get disheartened with your Paper 1 performance since you can never predict the results. Do not dilute your chance by compromising the CSAT paper.

I have discussed in the coming chapters the proper way to use those two hours between the two exams.

# 8

# What to Do to Get That Extra Edge in the Mains

It's the Mains that will determine whether you make it to the merit list or not. So, leaving this part for the two months after the Prelims is over-optimistic. If you want to secure a good rank, prepare beforehand.

**I have listed down the rules that worked for me in the Mains**

1. Memorize each word of the syllabus by heart. It becomes easier to know the demands of the examination as the syllabus has been defined appropriately. But most aspirants make the mistake of not going back to the syllabus again and again. Each topic that is mentioned is important, and you must be ready with

a 250 words write-up on it. In the actual exam, you'll have the base ready when a question on a particular topic comes up, and you just need to tweak it a bit as per the requirement of the question.

2. Understand what the question demands. Focus on the keywords and read the questions twice. Sometimes you may write beautifully, but without answering the question asked. If the question asks 'why', do not answer 'what' or 'how'. I was extremely cautious about this and hence underlined the keyword boldly as soon as I read the question. Know what each keyword means – critically analyse, enumerate, etc. This can help you a lot in keeping your answer to the point.

3. Address each part of the question. Every part carries equal marks. Hence make sure you read and allocate equal time and space to address all the subparts carefully.

4. Make notes beforehand. There are so many extra topics in the Mains syllabus that are not directly covered in the Prelims, like internal security, disaster management, NGOs, an entire paper of GS 4 and the optional subject. It is these topics that make a lot of difference in marks. I was determined not to leave everything for those three months after the Prelims, so I kept some time aside every weekend to read more about the topics on the Internet and

prepare comprehensive notes (with additions from newspapers). And I tried making the notes in an answer format, where the notes had an introduction, body and conclusion. This helped me to revise well in the last days and incorporate my notes directly into the answers.

The key takeaway is to go through at least 80–90 per cent of the Mains syllabus beforehand because it's always easy to process things when you have read them earlier with an open mind.

5. Write down the answers and attempt the mocks. As I have emphasized repeatedly, mocks are extremely crucial. In my first attempt, I kept waiting to have the perfect knowledge to write an ideal answer. It was a mistake. I realized later that it is practice that helps us reach closer to perfection.

   You should start answer-writing when you have a good hold on the basics and have read the subjects once. Don't wait for some extraordinary content or a good time to start writing.

6. Pay attention to the interconnection between subjects and sources. Irrespective of how much material is available, this habit of interconnecting facts cannot be spoon-fed. You will have to practise it mentally. This comes when you give yourself some time alone

away from the books and close your eyes to visualize whatever you have studied to date.

To simplify it, in the newspaper we come across so many case studies daily, some good examples of ethical work. The mistake we make is we keep noting such examples in a register that we aim to open at a later time. And even during the revision, we focus on cramming the facts. But the real benefit occurs when you go beyond that and fit an example or a case study mentally into some topic of GS or optional paper. This is what I mean by correlation.

I used to do this exercise a lot. Each time I saw new data, facts or anything happening around me, I quickly went back to the main syllabus mentally and tried to see where I could insert that observation to make my answer sound better.

And if something required frequent revisions, I would note it within the concerned topic instead of writing it on a different new page. Which data to fit where, is something you will learn with time and by developing the habit of mental analysis.

Let me simplify this with an example. I still remember a small news story – 'Indian Army sends back two girls with sweets and gifts who inadvertently crossed the LoC'. This piece of news could be used as an example in multiple topics of GS, like improving neighbourhood relations and goodwill among people, in the ethics paper and in essays. These small things make your answer stand out and reveal your creativity.

7. Cover multiple dimensions to write an answer. In the Mains exam, providing only a single dimension, say political, and explaining it comprehensively does not fetch enough marks. Instead, one must approach the answer from different angles like social, historical, environmental, ethical, economic, the security-related impact on India's foreign policy, etc., and provide a recent example or data to explain one's point further. Use the ARE approach – Assertion, Reasoning and Examples. This way, one's overall knowledge gets reflected in multiple spheres and one can incorporate the current news in one's answers too.

8. Revise, revise and then revise again. Very often we read multiple things but do not memorize them. In the actual exam, you might know a lot and yet very little when attempting an answer. The key to solving this problem is revision. Read the same books and notes multiple times, both for the Prelims and the Mains, rather than going to different sources repeatedly. I observed that during each revision I found a new point or understood the same concept from a different perspective, which helped add to

my depth of knowledge and made me truly remember the material.

Remember, the Mains is all about using your existing knowledge in the best possible way, knowing where to fit what and in which manner.

# 9

# How to Ace the Optional Subject

Though the sources, syllabus and books for every optional subject are different, a few rules apply to all optional subjects. The optional subject consists of two papers worth 500 marks, which means it has a huge weightage. These marks play a significant role in deciding your rank in the final list. So, it must be given adequate attention.

In my case, the following factors played an important role in choosing sociology as my optional.

1. My interest in the subject: You must not choose a subject that does not generate curiosity in your mind and an urge to know more. If you feel a subject is boring or tiring, do not choose it just because someone else secured a good rank with it in previous years. At the same time, choosing an optional solely based on your interest might be counterproductive. The end

goal should always be kept in mind, which is securing good marks and not becoming a professor of the subject.
2. Availability of material: As many subjects have to be studied for the UPSC, I did not want to waste a lot of time accumulating the right material. So, I wanted a subject whose sources were clear and whose toppers' strategies were easily available. The availability of notes covering the subject comprehensively was also crucial.
3. Length of the syllabus: If the syllabus is huge, it takes a lot of time to complete it from end to end. A short syllabus allows multiple revisions and a thorough understanding of the topics.

One thing that must not determine your choice is the marks scored by candidates from the previous years with different optional subjects. Every year the scenarios are different and there is no pattern as such followed by the UPSC. The marks are solely determined by individual efforts.

## How to prepare for optional subjects like sociology

The optional subject demands a depth of knowledge on every single topic. A brief reading of the topic is not sufficient. Cramming and rote learning of the theories without understanding also does not work. It's important to develop conceptual clarity, for which you might need to refer to multiple sources. So, do not panic if you cannot get everything in one place. First, try to have your concepts clear from whatever sources you are comfortable with, be it the notes available in the market or online videos on YouTube, etc. Then make sure to supplement it with standard books (that must be read thoroughly) and reference books (that can help with specific topics). Once you are done with the basics and start feeling comfortable with the subject, incorporate the points from all the sources in one place, which will be your standard 'go-to' source for revisions. I prepared my handwritten notes for every topic mentioned in the syllabus, making last-minute revisions very easy. You can even pick some available notes and write down the extra points in them.

Keep an eye out for optional-related material in the newspapers, specifically for dynamic subjects like political science and international relations, sociology and public administration. Correlating the theories of thinkers with current news becomes extremely important. I kept a special notebook for sociology-related current affairs and kept noting the relevant reports, case studies and examples to quote in the exam, especially in Paper 2, where direct questions are asked from the news.

When you write generic answers (not related to a particular thinker), quote thinkers who have different perspectives rather than writing multiple thinkers having the same ideology. For example, I made sure to include the perspectives of positivists and Marxist and feminist thinkers to add diverse viewpoints and then give a balanced conclusion in the end.

In the case of a very generic question, it becomes tricky to answer in a way that differentiates it from a simple general studies answer. To make my answer sound 'sociological', I incorporated the subheadings from the syllabus in my answer and explained them further. In optional subjects specifically, you cannot just assert the point but accompany it with proper reasoning to fetch good marks. Use examples, thinkers, case studies, facts and recent news to substantiate your point.

There is no hard and fast rule that thinkers stated in Paper 1 should not appear in Paper 2 and vice versa. I suggest you use them extensively since such examples depict your ability to correlate.

## 10

# How to Use the Two and a Half Months after the Prelims

I was very sceptical about clearing the Prelims – I had given myself a 50 per cent likelihood of doing so. But I didn't waste time waiting for the results. I started studying for the Mains. It is what one should ideally do. We cannot waste our time waiting for the results to be announced. I took a week's break to refresh and gather the energy to start with the Mains preparation.

The journey until the results are declared is anything but smooth. You constantly reel under the pressure and uncertainty of whether you will make it or not. But this is when you need to ride over it and keep studying.

As I had just taken the Prelims, the GS content was registered in my mind. So I decided to focus on the optional subject as I had not touched it since July. I started revising my notes, and within 10 days the results were announced and I had made it to the list. I started preparing wholeheartedly for the Mains.

I used the two months to revise self-made notes and did not focus a lot on reading new material. When you have cleared the Prelims, you have adequate knowledge, a conceptual base and a factual understanding of the topics. What becomes essential is the application of that knowledge, as discussed in the previous chapter. I focused on revising the current affairs notes I had prepared from the Mains perspective, reading newspapers and the static notes on a few extra topics from GS papers, besides an extensive revision of the sociology notes.

I immediately joined the GS Mains test series after the Prelims results. I had already joined the sociology test series in June. I started giving part tests, syllabus-wise (in which only a limited portion of the syllabus is asked), after adequate revision.

As I had not attempted a three-hour GS paper (GS 1, 2, 3) even once, I faced issues completing it on time, but eventually, with adequate practice, my speed became good. I made sure to analyse my performance in each test, self-evaluate the answers, work on the feedback given by evaluators and borrow some relevant points from the model answers.

In sociology, I watched the entire test discussion,

which helped me add some good examples and clarify my concepts even better. In the first half of December, my preparation took a turn for the worse, as mentioned in the earlier chapters, due to my grandpa's condition.

By the second half of that month, I was running behind schedule, and it took me some time to return to that 'full preparation' mode. When I was back on track, in the last two weeks, I made short notes for each paper, consisting of data to be quoted and facts and diagrams that could be incorporated into the questions. In the last week, I gave mocks in the school setting.

The rules for the day before the exam remain the same as for the Prelims. A day before, I read some quotations for the essay paper. It becomes extremely important to plan the two hours between the two exams cautiously; you cannot let your energy go low in the second half. I have discussed this in the next chapter. The Mains is a good five-day process with five days in between, making it 10 days in total. Mental grit plays a significant role in sailing through this exam. I have already discussed in Part 1 how sheer mental toughness is needed to overcome the on-day challenges.

# 11

# How to Use the Two Hours between the Two Mains Papers

Every minute in those two hours becomes crucial, as you need to re-energize your mind and body for another three-hour-long paper. Make sure you don't waste time discussing the paper with fellow aspirants, irrespective of your performance. You must concentrate and focus on giving the best possible performance in the next exam.

**So quickly find your way out of the exam hall, avoid gossiping with anyone and make sure to carry an umbrella.** During my exam, it was continuously pouring, and some candidates had to wait for someone to bring an umbrella. It wastes a lot of time, so make sure you are not dependent on others for these small but crucial items.

After exiting the exam hall, do not waste time searching for your parents. Decide beforehand the location you will meet them. My brother made sure he was there to receive me at the gate and my father waited in the car to save the time it took to drive out of the parking area.

Outside the exam hall, parking can be an issue and if you have your own vehicle it may waste a lot of your time. My father, therefore, made sure to reach an hour early and get a decent spot to park the car away from the traffic, and it saved some 5–10 minutes. I observed that many cars were stuck in the traffic due to rain, so these minor things need to be kept in mind.

If you stay close to the exam hall, you save travel time. As soon as you enter the vehicle, you should replenish yourself with an energy drink and some glucose-rich food. It could be packaged juice or chocolate, or both. I had coffee as it was wintertime – my father and brother got coffee in the thermos and a hot water bottle to ease the pain in my fingers, swollen from continuous writing.

We reached our place in about eight minutes. Then I had a good meal. Kindly do not skip your lunch, as your body and mind must work coherently during the exam. Avoid rice or fried items so you don't feel sleepy during the exam. After lunch and a nap of about 15–20 minutes, I revised my last-minute notes quickly. Before leaving for the exam hall, I had coffee to feel fully active.

The two-hour interval had ended, and there I was sitting in the exam hall again, ready to fight another three-hour battle. However, remember that things won't always go as per the plan. As I had mentioned earlier, I was sick during one of my exams and only took medicines and lemon water. I couldn't eat anything and could not revise anything, so it's fine to not have the ideal circumstances. This, in no way, should let any self-doubt creep in. Kabhi kissi ko mukamaal jahan nahin milta! (No one ever gets the entire world!)

## 12

# Acing the Interview Stage

The Interview is the last stage of this long journey and holds a weightage of 275 marks, which is not an insignificant chunk. Most aspirants misunderstand the Interview to be a 'speaking skills' test and start paying too much attention to their style of speaking, fluency and eloquence, completely neglecting the actual demand of this stage. The stage is referred to as the 'personality test', which speaks enough of the demand. The respected panellists ask questions not just to test your knowledge or crammed facts but your personality, which reflects in your answers. Let's see the rules of this stage:

1. Be honest in your Detailed Application Form (or the DAF, that you submit after clearing the Mains). The first step to ace the Interview is to fill out the DAF carefully. The DAF is a document where you have to fill in your interests, hobbies, extracurriculars, educational

background, etc. A major part of your personality will be reflected in this document, even before you speak a single word. You must not try to make it 'interesting' by putting things you haven't done. You must be 100 per cent confident about whatever you write in the DAF. Do not mention a hobby just because it could seem appealing or push the panellists to ask questions. Trust me, you will not be able to answer the questions if you don't truly pursue that hobby. Your integrity and honesty will be checked there itself, and if you fail in that aspect, your chances of getting through this stage become negligible.

2. Work on your content. It is a myth that you need not read or study extra for this stage. What you speak matters more than how you speak. And specifically, in the questions that lend themselves to debate, you must know the arguments of both sides well enough to be able to justify your stance. You must prepare on every keyword from your DAF. This exploration makes this stage very interesting too. I used to enjoy framing new questions every day from my DAF and then reading up about what I wrote in the answers in depth. Be thorough with the regional, national and international news. Revise your optional subject and correlate the theory with current affairs. I read a lot during those two months before the interview and even made

comprehensive notes on all the keywords in my DAF, like my place of birth; schooling; questions related to my parents' profession; major issues in my state, historical, cultural and environmental importance of my city; etc. The content for this stage is very open-ended and less bookish.

3. Practise speaking. If you fear speaking in front of others, ensure you practise thoroughly. Ask your family members or friends to take a 10-minute mock interview daily. I encouraged my family members to ask me questions whenever they were free. It helped me explain myself in a few words, and control my speed too; earlier, I spoke too fast. This daily routine goes a long way in boosting your confidence.

4. Go for mock interviews. While mock interviews are helpful, I suggest not going overboard as you might lose the originality and freshness of your answers. I appeared in about six to seven offline mock interviews. I did not attend any online interviews as I felt they did not serve my purpose. My intent to appear in mocks was to come out of my comfort zone and get accustomed to facing four or five senior panellists.

The kind of pressure you learn to handle in an offline interview cannot be matched by a virtual one. So, I travelled to Delhi three times and managed about two mocks in a day. Make sure you work on the feedback before appearing for another interview. Do not get discouraged by negative feedback. Remember the actual interview will always go differently. Just prepare for the questions that you were unable to answer.

5. Practise in formal attire. You must be comfortable with your attire and know how to carry it well on the day of the interview. If you are not used to wearing a saree (for women) or a formal suit (for men), practise doing so multiple times.

6. Be positive and balanced in your answers. It becomes crucial to have an optimistic outlook in your answers. You must not be too critical or too rigid in your approach. Be flexible enough to mould your stance as per the situation. In controversial questions, take a stand in coherence with the Constitutional principles. In situational questions, like your response to a disaster, be practical. Know what powers and responsibilities are attached to a particular authority, and do not commit to something that is beyond your reach.

7. Be extremely honest. Saying 'yes' to every question and not being able to answer is a risky call. It's perfectly fine to politely say 'no' when you do not know the answer. Be confident about what you know and have an attitude of learning from the things you do not know. Even if it means six or seven consecutive 'nos'

as your answers, it is perfectly fine. Many aspirants succumb to the pressure when they cannot answer a few questions, and ultimately, afraid to say no, they give a wrong answer. It is counterproductive and gives a very wrong impression to the panellists. Do not try to fool them because you cannot and you must not do so.

8. Be confident: Remind yourself that you have cleared the two stages, which testifies that you have adequate knowledge and you have what it takes to clear the Interview. Hence, you must walk inside the hall with confidence and with a spirit to learn something new from some very experienced senior members.

# Epilogue

If you are reading this, it shows that you are hell-bent on cracking the UPSC or any other challenging exam. Each reader will get their own particular insights from this book, but I hope you have learnt that even with the best of intentions, your hard work must be fine-tuned with time-tested strategies if you want to succeed.

If there is one thing I would ask you, my reader, it is to do thorough and honest soul-searching to identify your particular lacunae in strategy, vulnerable points and scope of improvement. Only you are the best judge of that. Maybe some of you are burdening yourself with unnecessary comparisons with your peers; others might be overworking without properly designed breaks or compromising their mental and physical capacities. Some might be taking too much pressure from family, friends, mentors; others might be overstressing or feeling too much guilt. Some of you might not be planning enough or working with consistency. It is only via thorough

## Epilogue

introspection that you will find the gaps, like allowing yourself too many excuses, overrating the circumstances, overlooking the importance of mock tests or PYQs, or not giving the requisite importance to each stage of the exam.

If I can go from failing by a huge margin in the very first stage to successfully scaling all the three stages, and bagging an all India Rank 3 – you can too. But I must reiterate that you have to be honest with yourself while smartly utilizing the experiences and proven strategies reflected from my own accounts and the indispensable Rules of the Game which I have set out in this book. Then I can assure you that you will find new vigour, strength and self-confidence to scale any hurdle.

The last thing I would like to suggest is to focus on the process and enjoy the journey fully. When you look back at these preparation days, they are going to be the most memorable ones irrespective of the results you achieve, and the learnings will stay with you throughout.

ALL THE BEST to each one of you. May your dreams come true!

# Appendix

**Here is the book list I followed:**

1. Modern history: *A Brief History of Modern India* by Rajiv Ahir (Spectrum Books Pvt Ltd.)
2. Ancient history: *Our Pasts*, Part 1 (Class VI, NCERT); *Ancient Indian History* by R.S. Sharma (Class XI, NCERT)
3. Medieval history: *Our Pasts*, Part 2 (Class VII, NCERT); *History of Medieval India* by Satish Chandra (Class XI, NCERT)
4. World history (Mains – GS 1): *Indian and Contemporary World* – I (Class IX, NCERT); *Indian and Contemporary World* – II (Class X, NCERT); Section 4 from *Themes in World History* (Class XI, NCERT)
5. Geography: Textbooks of Class X, XI and XII, NCERT; *Certificate Physical and Human Geography* by G.C. Leong (Oxford University Press); an atlas for map work

6. Polity: *Indian Polity* by M. Lakshmikant; *Political Theory* (Class XI, NCERT)
7. Art and culture: *An Introduction to Indian Art*, Part 1 (Class XI, NCERT); *Indian Art and Culture* by Nitin Singhania (McGraw Hill)
8. Economics: *Indian Economic Development* (Class XI, NCERT); *Introductory Macroeconomics* (Class XII, NCERT); chapter summary of Economic Survey 2021; summary of Union Budget 2021
9. Environment and biodiversity: *Environment* (Shankar IAS); biology textbooks of class XI and XII (NCERT, only some chapters)
10. Science and technology; defence: Mainly relied on current affairs

Along with these standard books, I covered current affairs for each subject from *The Hindu* and through daily news analysis on online websites.

## The syllabus:

The syllabus of GS 1 includes the following topics:
- Current events of national and international importance

## Appendix

- History of India and the Indian national movement
- Indian and world geography – physical, social, economic geography of India and the world
- Indian polity and governance – Constitution, political system, the Panchayati Raj, public policy, rights issues, etc.
- Economic and social development – sustainable development, poverty, inclusion, demographics, social sector initiatives, etc.
- General issues on environmental ecology, biodiversity and climate change that do not require subject specialization
- General science

The syllabus of CSAT paper includes the following topics:
- Comprehension
- Interpersonal skills including communication skills
- Logical reasoning and analytical ability
- Decision-making and problem-solving
- General mental ability
- Basic numeracy (numbers and their relations, orders of magnitude, etc.; Class X level)
- Data interpretation (charts, graphs, tables, data sufficiency etc.; Class X level)

## Appendix

The syllabus of the Mains paper is mentioned in brief below:

1. Paper A – Compulsory Indian language (I chose Punjabi)
2. Paper B – English
3. Paper I – Essay (two long essays)
4. Paper II (General Studies I) – Indian Heritage & Culture; History & Geography of the World & Society
5. Paper III (General Studies II) – Governance, Constitution, Welfare Initiatives, Social Justice & International Relations
6. Paper IV (General Studies III) – Technology, Economic Development, Agriculture, Biodiversity, Security & Disaster Management
7. Paper V (General Studies IV) – Ethics, Integrity & Aptitude
8. Paper VI – Optional Subject – Paper I
9. Paper VII – Optional Subject – Paper II

Appendix

# My marksheet:

## Marks I received in the UPSE Mains examination (2021)

| Subjects | Marks |
|---|---|
| Essay Paper – I | 117 |
| General Studies – I (Paper – II) | 98 |
| General Studies – II (Paper – III) | 129 |
| General Studies – III (Paper – IV) | 103 |
| General Studies – IV (Paper – V) | 124 |
| Optional – I (Sociology) (Paper – VI) | 154 |
| Optional – II (Sociology) (Paper – VII) | 133 |
| Written Total | 858 |
| Personality Test | 187 |
| Final Total | 1045 |

**Source:** From the archives of the UPSC online marksheet system at https://upsconline.nic.in/marksheet/exam/marksheet_system/archives.php

# Acknowledgements

I believe that my achievements are due to the blessings of God, heartfelt wishes of elders and friends, and the support of my family. I am fortunate to have received all these in abundance. Writing a book is exciting, intriguing, challenging and satisfying – all at the same time – and it wouldn't have been possible without some fabulous people in my life.

I can't thank my parents, Dr Alok Singla and Dr Neeraj Singla, enough for believing in me, especially during the times I didn't believe in myself. They backed every decision of mine and were by my side come what may. And their constant valuable feedback while I was writing the book not only boosted my confidence but also helped me course correct as and when needed. I am indebted to my beloved father for helping me in finalizing the drafts after multiple readings.

My heartfelt gratitude to my brother, Tushar Singla, a graduate from IIT Kharagpur, currently working as a

## Acknowledgements

software engineer with Cisco, Bengaluru, for encouraging me to go ahead with this idea of sharing my experiences with aspirants. He was a constant support throughout and made me realize my true potential, everytime I tried settling for less.

To my grandmother, Smt. Nirmala Devi Singla for her constant prayers for my good health and well-being and unconditional love. To my Nana and late Nani for their invaluable blessings always.

To my uncle, Ankur Singla, who was amongst the first few persons I discussed the idea of writing this book. His confidence in me and the idea pushed me to pursue it. I thank him for helping me at every stage of this book – in finding a good publisher, in guiding me on how to start writing the drafts, in editing and then finalizing the book.

I am deeply grateful to Chiki Sarkar for trusting me with this book. Being a first-time author, I found her constant guidance truly valuable. I'm grateful to her and the talented Juggernaut team, who have been a true support and have helped me improve my drafts immensely.

Last but not the least, thanks to all the UPSC CSE aspirants whose multiple requests regarding different aspects of this preparation helped answer all their queries and cover different aspects of preparation at one place.

# A Note on the Author

Gamini Singla did her graduation in BTech Computer Science from Punjab Engineering College, Chandigarh in 2019. Post that, she started her UPSC preparation and secured all India Rank 3 in CSE in her second attempt in 2021. Currently, she is undergoing training as an IAS officer.